# Achieving tl
# New Internati
# Quality Stand

# Achieving the New International Quality Standards

*A Step-by-step Guide to BS EN ISO9000*

■

**LESLEY MUNRO-FAURE,
MALCOLM MUNRO-FAURE**
and
**EDWARD BONES**

*the Institute
of Management*

FOUNDATION

PITMAN
PUBLISHING

PITMAN PUBLISHING
128 Long Acre, London WC2E 9AN

A Division of Pearson Professional Limited

First published as *Achieving Quality Standards* 1993

This edition published Great Britain 1995

© Munro Associates 1995

*British Library Cataloguing in Publication Data*
A CIP catalogue record for this book can be obtained
from the British Library

ISBN 0 273 61977 2

3  5  7  9  10  8  6  4  2

Typeset by Northern Phototypesetting Co. Ltd, Bolton
Printed and bound in Great Britain by
Bell and Bain Ltd, Glasgow

*The Publishers' policy is to use paper manufactured
from sustainable forests.*

# Contents

■

vi

## APPENDICES

# Foreword

■

An effective Quality Management System actively works to improve business performance. This is achieved by understanding customer requirements, and then controlling your business to ensure those requirements are met first time, every time. The framework set out in the International Standard for Quality Management Systems, ISO9000, provides a sound basis for a Quality Management System.

Some managers have come to believe that developing a Quality Management System to meet this standard will act as a bureaucratic straitjacket and an obstacle to improved business performance.

This book explodes that myth. Companies with a costly, bureaucratic Quality Management System frequently blame the standard. They should not. The real blame rests with themselves. It is they who have developed and implemented their system badly.

This book describes how you can avoid this pitfall by developing an effective Quality Management System. Using this book will help you control your business. The practical guidance will provide an invaluable aid to managers. It will enable you to develop and implement a Quality Management System which will lead to improved performance. It will also lead to increased customer satisfaction, reduced waste and inefficiency, improved profitability and employee morale.

Roger Young
Director General of the Institute of Management

# Munro Associates

■

Munro Associates is an established management consultancy which specialises in helping companies learn how to really benefit from implementing quality management techniques. Our partners have experience of working in manufacturing and service organisations across a wide range of industries. We have built up a considerable body of experience about how to apply the quality management approach to give a better understanding of customer needs and produce a real improvement in performance. We focus on helping businesses to utilise internal resources to develop ownership of the system and to lead the improvement effort.

Munro Associates
11 Bolton Street
London W1Y 7PA

Telephone (44) 0171 408 1035
Fax (44) 0171 408 1048

# Introduction
# Implementing BS EN ISO9000

■

Quality is the key to achieving customer satisfaction.

In today's highly competitive marketplace many organisations offer broadly the same range of products or services. The principal differentiating factor in the eyes of customers is frequently the Quality of the total service offered. Quality of the delivered product or service is essential, but this is the minimum requirement. It is the quality of your overall relationship with your customers that counts.

Quality can also reduce your operating costs. Surveys show that businesses frequently waste as much as 25 per cent of turnover on ineffective or inefficient processes which result in errors and waste. A Quality organisation focuses on understanding and controlling its activities so they do not produce errors or waste.

An effective Quality Management System has a key role to play in improving your business performance because:

- you will understand your customers' requirements
- you will know how to satisfy their requirements
- you will understand how to organise and control your business to minimise errors and waste
- you will improve profitability and competitiveness.

This book explains how your business can reap the benefits of an effective Quality Management System. BS EN ISO9000 is an international series of standards which define the basic features of an effective Quality Management System. BS EN ISO9000 was revised and updated in 1994; it is recognised in the UK (BS), Europe (EN) and Internationally (ISO). The previous UK Standard, BS5750 no longer exists. Throughout the book we will refer to ISO9000; this should be taken to mean the particular element of the ISO9000 series of quality standards which applies to your business. The book is divided into three key sections:

(i)   a senior management guide to Quality Management and ISO9000 describing the benefits of an effective Quality Management System and the commitment required to succeed in Chapters 1 to 3;

(ii) a practical step-by-step guide on how to implement an effective Quality Management System which meets the needs of your business, the needs of your customers and the requirements of ISO9000, in Chapters 4 to 12; and

(iii) the appendices contain examples of the key documents which form the basis of an effective Quality Management System to provide a starting point for your own system.

Our purpose in this book it not to tell you how to implement your Quality Management System. Every business is unique and so each QMS is unique. Only you can define and implement a system which meets your needs and enables you to achieve your business objectives.

Our purpose is to give you a vision of the benefits an effective QMS can bring and guide you through what is required. We have given you examples of what has worked in other organisations. It is up to you to design a system that works for your business. You will succeed if you are really committed to understanding and managing your business for total customer satisfaction and maximum profitability.

ISO9000 applies equally to all businesses: service or manufacturing, hi-tech or traditional. This creates a potential language barrier. To overcome this we have used functional terms throughout the text. Every business may have a different name for these activities. It is important to identify the groups within your organisation who are tasked with the functions described. Some examples are given in the table below.

**Examples of names used in different organisations to describe key business functions**

| Manufacturing | Accounting firm | Hospital |
| --- | --- | --- |
| Design | Audit and tax technical groups responsible for designing new client services | Hospital consultants<br>Hospital managers |
| Production | Audit and tax managers and staff who are responsible for 'doing the work' | Hospital staff<br>– doctors<br>– nurses<br>– administration |
| Marketing | Marketing groups, specialist technical groups | Hospital managers responsible for agreeing contracts with Health authorities and budget holders<br><br>Consultants who have developed a leading reputation |
| Sales | Partners and managers tasked with selling services to clients | Hospital managers<br>Consultants |

# 1

# What is Quality?
# An introduction to ISO9000

- ■ **What is Quality?**
- ■ **Quality costs: a driving force**
- ■ **The Quality Management System**
- ■ **Benefits of a certified Quality Management System**
- ■ **Implementing your Quality Management System**

## What is Quality?

There is only one focal point in business today: *your customers*. Quality is defined by customers. First of all, you need to agree what your customers want (their requirements), then you must produce exactly what is wanted within the agreed timeframe at minimum cost. The Quality concept is not difficult to understand, but it does require attention from everyone.

The customers of the organisation are not merely those who purchase your products or services, they are everyone for whom the organisation works. This includes those who purchase products or services those who use them and the owners or shareholders of the organisation. Take the case of a hospital Trust; customers include the Health authority and other Trusts which purchase services, patients and visitors who use those services and the trust board, on behalf of government and tax payers (the 'shareholders'), which is responsible for ensuring the pro-fitability of the organisation. The interests of all these customers have much in common; they all wish to see the organisation work efficiently and effectively, at minimum cost. By considering all interests, the 1994 ISO9000 Standard permits the development of a Quality Management System which can be simple, cost effective and efficient, addressing the needs of all customers of the business.

'Quality' is not only concerned with whether a product or service meets the claims made for it. Your customer's perception of your business is based on the product or service you deliver and on the day-to-day contact he has with you and your staff. The Quality concept embraces how you meet *all* your customers' requirements, including how they are greeted on the telephone; the speed with which salesmen respond to a request for a quotation; having new products and services when required and even ensuring the invoice is correct! Every contact with every customer on every occasion builds a picture of your company in the eyes of your customers.

The receptionist who answers telephone calls, the security people who control access to the site, the accounts clerk who sends out the invoice can all have a direct and important influence on customers. Everyone must be involved in Quality; in meeting customer requirements; in creating a world-class company.

Customers demand that your products and services conform to their requirements first time every time. Quality can therefore be defined as achieving conformance to requirements first time every time. By adopting this definition of Quality you will be able to measure, assess and improve the performance of your business. Quality is an objective concept. It is something that the whole workforce can understand and measure, and for which they can accept responsibility.

## THE KEY TO MEETING CUSTOMER REQUIREMENTS

Modern businesses are generally complex and split into different departments such as:

- *marketing* – the people who determine customer requirements
- *selling* – the people who ensure your products and services are purchased
- *design and development* – the people who develop tomorrow's products and services
- *production* – the people who actually produce and deliver the service to the customer
- *purchasing* – the people who buy-in external products and services to support your ability to service your customers
- *finance and administration* – the people who ensure that the company's finances are prudently managed

- *after-sales support* – the people who support customers in their use of the product or service after delivery.

How can you ensure all these departments pull together to meet the requirements of your external customers?

Your salesmen will identify the requirements of your customers. The production department relies on the information from the salesman to define its output. It also relies on the purchasing department for raw materials, equipment and services. Finance relies on information from sales and production to raise the invoice. A breakdown in any one of these internal chains may result in an error which will affect the service received by your external customer. The ability to meet external customer requirements relies on a series of, often complex, internal supplier/customer chains.

Quality must involve each of these internal chains if external customers are to receive only conforming goods or services. No one is exempt. You must ensure that errors in every internal supplier/customer chain are eliminated if you are to satisfy external customer requirements at minimum cost. The only way to achieve this is to:

3

(i)   understand the requirements of your external customers;

(ii)  understand the internal processes which enable you to meet these requirements; and

(iii) develop a system and culture which ensures errors are eliminated.

## Quality costs – a driving force

Your business, in common with many others, is probably wasting large sums of money because of an inability to carry out the right tasks, right first time. Most companies spend significant amounts of time and money doing the wrong things and also putting things right after they have gone wrong. The costs associated with these activities can amount to 25 per cent of turnover. These are the costs associated with failure to achieve conformance to requirements and are generally termed non-conformance costs. Eliminating this unnecessary burden will enable you to improve profitability in the short term and enhance competitiveness in the longer term. These non-conformance costs are, however, not merely the costs associated with getting things wrong, they also arise through doing the wrong things. The objective of any well-managed business is 'to do the right things' and then to 'do things right'.

Non-conformance costs may arise in any department. All departments spend some time doing unnecessary activities; correcting their own mistakes, or rectifying other people's errors. Consequently all departments will benefit from Quality Improvement. No one is exempt.

As ISO9000 is increasingly adopted by service organisations the activities traditionally associated with a manufacturing approach to Quality are being re-thought. For example, within manufacturing organisations there was traditionally thought to be a need to carry out independent inspection of work at various points throughout the manufacturing process. Indeed, in some service organisations these types of activities also take place. This policy creates a cost which must be justified against the benefits and alternatives considered before this is enshrined in the practices of the organisation. Independent inspection is often found to be an unnecessary activity, a cost of non-conformance. There is no requirement in the Standard to carry out this activity and it should be eliminated wherever the costs of implementation outweigh the benefits it brings.

4

Many companies are aware of direct product and service-related failure costs as they give rise to professional indemnity or warranty claims, scrap and rework. However, most businesses ignore the vast amounts of money they waste in other areas. The costs of rework in administration areas, the costs associated with excessive debtor days, or the costs incurred when customer requirements haven't been fully determined. All these factors need to be controlled.

Many businesses try to prevent the supply of defective product to customers by operating extensive appraisal activities. Here, the output from every process is checked. This can mean products or services are checked at many stages during their journey through the organisation. This appraisal activity, and its associated cost, is only necessary because the system produces so many errors. These have to be found and corrected. If you could only identify the causes of failure and eliminate them by introducing prevention activities, you could slash the costs of this appraisal activity.

A relatively small investment in prevention activities (such as planning, effective procedures, training, calibration or equipment maintenance) can reduce the burden of both failure and appraisal costs. Eliminating the causes of failure will increase profitability and significantly improve the service you provide to your customers.

The objective of a Quality Management System (QMS) is to improve

Quality by eliminating the causes of non-conformance in every activity throughout the company. Everyone, starting with management, should refuse to accept the inevitability of errors and concentrate on preventing them occurring in the first place.

The benefits which can accrue from implementating a successful QMS are enormous:

- improved customer satisfaction
- elimination of errors and waste
- reduced operating costs
- increased motivation and commitment from employees
- increased profitability and competitiveness.

Indeed the very survival of the company itself may be at stake. If you are unable to sort out your business, then your competitors may do it for you.

# The Quality Management System

5

The Quality Management System (QMS) defines the Quality environment within a business. Every business is different and so each QMS will be unique. An effective QMS can be developed for any type of business, whether service or manufacturing, high-tech or traditional. The common features are:

(i)   it must be based on understanding your business, your customers and their requirements;

(ii)  it must be management led;

(iii) it must involve all employees in its implementation;

(iv)  it must focus on preventing errors rather than merely detecting and correcting them. This minimises the overall cost burden and improves business performance; and

(v)   it must be able to evolve as the company itself changes and develops.

A successful QMS is a management system which enables *you* to ensure customer requirements are understood and met first time, every time, at minimum cost to the business.

A Quality Management System embraces all areas of the organisation: marketing, contract acceptance, product design, production, delivery, service, finance and administration. The objective of the QMS is to ensure only conforming products and services reach your customers. A successful QMS establishes control over all business processes. It must be flexible and evolve to ensure it continues to meet the changing needs of the customers and your organisation.

## QUALITY SYSTEM STANDARDS – THEIR DEVELOPMENT AND CURRENT ROLE

The development of QMS standards in the UK can be traced back to the late 1950s and early 1960s. At this time the Ministry of Defence (MoD) recognised that control of key processes by its suppliers would reduce the level, and hence the cost, of field equipment failures. This led to the development of a series of defence standards. These described the basic business processes over which a supplier had to develop documented controls to provide assurance that only conforming products would be delivered. Because of its background, this series of standards focused primarily on manufacturing industries; on defence suppliers; and on assuring product conformance.

In the 1970s, these defence standards were incorporated into, and replaced by, AQAP standards. These were quality system standards operated and recognised by NATO countries for suppliers in the defence industry. Registration and assessment against these standards was carried out by the MoD in the UK. Registration was only available for businesses which were, or were expected to become, suppliers to the MoD.

As the benefits of quality systems became apparent both to customers (by assuring the delivery of conforming goods) and to suppliers (by improving customer satisfaction and reducing operating costs) the need became recognised for a Quality System Standard which could be used by industry in general. This led to the development in the UK of the British Standard, BS5750, in 1979. This standard was largely based on the NATO AQAP series of standards. Any organisation could be assessed and registered if it satisfied the assessing body that its Quality Management System met the requirements of BS5750.

In 1987, a number of nations ratified an agreement recognising an International Quality System Standard, the ISO9000 series. This was a direct equivalent of BS5750 (1987) and was widely recognised throughout the world.

In summer 1994 the ISO9000 series of Standards was revised and reissued. The new standard, BS EN ISO9000 is widely recognised throughout the world. The original UK equivalent standard no longer exists, it has been superseded by the new document. The 1994 revision of the Standard follows the basic philosophy and structure of the 1987 version; it does, however, include some new requirements, clarifies some points and makes explicit some requirements which were previously implicit. The ISO9000 series is the leading international quality system standard today.

Because of the nature of its development from the original defence standards, BS5750 and subsequently ISO9000 were initially written primarily from a manufacturing and product assurance viewpoint. This has made interpretation more difficult for service industries. Initially, therefore, a relatively small number of (mainly manufacturing) companies were registered as conforming to the standard.

Because the standards have to be applied across a wide range of industry and commerce, their requirements are often stated in very general terms. As a result, a number of industry-specific guidelines have been developed by the British Standards Institute (BSI) and appropriate industry representatives. These expand and interpret specific clauses in the standards. They provide detailed guidance which is useful in applying the standard to particular business sectors. They are, however, only guidelines. They are not part of the standard itself and do not form part of the basis for assessment.

The development of these guidelines, and the 1994 revision of the Standard have led to an increased understanding of the application of the standards within service industries. This, together with the recognition of the growing importance of Quality as a basis for competitive advantage, has led to a rapid increase in the number of businesses applying for ISO9000 approval. The number of organisations registered as conforming to ISO9000 has grown from 5,000 in 1983 to over 15,000 in 1995. This total includes many service organisations such as solicitors, accountants, educational establishments and health service units.

Customers are increasingly expecting their suppliers to operate a Quality Management System to provide assurance that they will only receive conforming products and services. The independent approval of a company's Quality Management System (QMS) to an internationally recognised Standard, such as ISO9000, demonstrates that a company takes customer requirements seriously and has implemented a system to recognise and ensure conformance to those requirements.

# Benefits of a certified Quality Management System

An approved QMS provides assurance to customers that the company is committed to Quality. It demonstrates that the supplier has implemented procedures which enable it to:

- identify the requirements of its customers
- ensure it is able to supply products and services in accordance with those requirements
- ensure delivered products conform to those requirements.

The standards only define what must be controlled. They do not specify how that control is to be achieved. A company which understands *why* it is introducing a QMS can implement a flexible system which suits its business needs. It is then in a position to realise the benefits which an effective QMS can bring.

8

An effective QMS will ensure that the activities of the business are understood, controlled and documented. This enables everyone to know what they are doing and how to do it. As a result, inefficiencies and waste may be targeted and eliminated.

The benefits of an effective QMS are many but they can only be realised by a company which recognises them, is committed to Quality, and takes the time and trouble to devise a well-thought out system which advances its business objectives.

The following are typical of the benefits of a well planned QMS:

(i) satisfied and loyal customers because goods and services are always produced according to their requirements;

(ii) reduced operating costs as waste is eliminated and efficiency increased as a result of eliminating non-conformance;

(iii) improved competitiveness and profitability as operating costs are reduced; and

(iv) improved morale as employees develop greater understanding of the business, are able to work efficiently, and are involved in managing their working environment.

Many organisations fail to reap these benefits because management do not take into account the requirements of their business when implementing their QMS. This might happen if, for example, the company implements a QMS because of pressure from a major customer to seek ISO9000 approval. Unless the QMS is adequately planned the real benefits of an effective system may not be realised.

In the worst case, you could finish up with a system that is inflexible, difficult to manage and does not advance your commercial objectives. This type of system may well result if you relinquish ownership of your QMS and leave it to be designed and implemented by an external consultant. An inflexible QMS is usually seen to be a waste of time with no real benefits for your business.

It is important to avoid falling into the trap of implementing a QMS without paying adequate attention to your overall business needs and objectives. A QMS should actively improve business performance, not act as an obstacle! What you really need is a living, breathing system which evolves with your business. You will only achieve this if you are closely involved in defining and implementing your QMS.

9

## DO YOU NEED EXTERNAL ASSESSMENT AND REGISTRATION?

An effective QMS can be implemented without external assessment and registration against a Quality System Standard. However, in addition to providing information and guidance on how an effective QMS should operate, independent assessment has significant commercial benefits:

(i)   it provides evidence to customers that the QMS has been independently assessed as effective. This is increasingly important as a marketing edge over competitors;

(ii)  it avoids duplication of customer assessments. Most customers accept and recognise ISO9000 approval. This saves time and money for both the customer and supplier. The companies can then concentrate on satisfying specific requirements for particular contracts or orders; and

(iii) it provides evidence of a responsible attitude to Quality, and to product and service liability requirements. This can be used as a basis to limit indemnity insurance costs.

## WHAT IS THE ROLE OF MANAGEMENT?

Employees are a mirror of their management. Employees generally perform according to what they believe their managers require of them.

This is why Quality must be management led. If you want your employees to believe that your business is focused on:

- understanding and meeting customer needs
- understanding the business processes
- investing time and effort in preventing errors

then you will have to convince them that this is what you want.

Your role is vital. Only senior management are able to change the philosophy and culture of your organisation:

- you must ensure your aims are understood by everyone in the business
- you must demonstrate your commitment to these aims by your daily actions and words
- you must encourage your employees to become actively involved in ensuring a successful QMS is developed to meet those business aims.

Thus, management has five key roles:

(i)   determine the aims of your business, its philosophy and policy for Quality;

(ii)  develop a QMS to ensure this policy is understood and implemented at all levels;

(iii) encourage every employee to become involved in implementing the QMS;

(iv)  invest the necessary skills and resources to ensure the QMS is effective; and

(v)   take an active role in implementing and developing the QMS.

Chapter 4 describes in more detail how to fulfil these roles and ensure the implementation of an effective Quality Management System.

## WHY DOES EVERYONE NEED TO BE INVOLVED?

You are probably the best person to describe what you do at work; what problems you face and what could be done to enable you to work more effectively. The same is probably true of everyone. Your receptionist probably knows what prevents her from answering the phone within three rings; office staff will know what problems they face because of poor filing or time recording systems. They could also probably tell you what would help them overcome these problems, even if they do not have the complete answer. To implement a successful QMS, it is important to harness the skills and enthusiasm of everyone in the business. You will want to find out how to enable everyone to improve their performance so you can meet your customers' requirements at minimum cost. To achieve this, individuals must be provided with the skills, tools and authority to make the necessary changes. Managers must also demonstrate that they believe their employees can make an important contribution to their working environment. If you can create an open atmosphere you will help this to happen. Teamwork will be the key to successful businesses in the 1990s and beyond. This radical change will only happen if it is actively and passionately led from the top. It cannot happen overnight and it is unlikely to be painless, unless it is carefully managed.

## THE REQUIREMENTS OF THE ISO9000 STANDARDS

There are three major parts within the ISO9000 series against which your QMS can be developed and assessed:

ISO9001 – model for Quality Assurance in design, development, production, installation and servicing.

ISO9002 – model for Quality Assurance in production and installation.

ISO9003 – model for Quality Assurance in final inspection and test.

Generally, ISO9003 applies *only* if assurance of conformance to requirements can be determined purely by inspection or test of the complete item. This standard is very rarely the most appropriate basis for a QMS. It is generally necessary to control other processes to ensure conformance to customer requirements at minimum cost. It is not usually adequate, or cost effective, to rely solely on final inspection and test for this purpose.

ISO9002 covers all the processes common to those businesses which carry out manufacture and delivery of a product or service but which are not involved in the original design of that product or service.

ISO9001, which is the most comprehensive of the standards, covers the requirements of ISO9002 and also the controls necessary over design activities. The Standard applies equally to the design of products or services. It applies where the design itself (in the form of specifications, reports or drawings) are delivered to the customer, or where the supplier produces the product or service and then delivers this to the customer.

Service design could apply to any instance when a new service is generated. It can be a service generated for a specific client such as the design of a maintenance schedule, or a specific training course. Alternatively the design could cover a service which will be marketed and sold to a range of customers, for instance the design of a new banking service, or the design of a training package.

The appropriate Standard to apply depends on the activities of the company. The requirements of the standards are compared in Fig 1.1. Guidance notes in the introduction to each Standard, and in the guidance document, ISO9000, help in the selection of the appropriate level. The accredited assessment bodies will also provide advice to applicants on the appropriate standard. A list of the certification bodies is included in Appendix 11.

Each Standard defines the activities for which a company must provide appropriate controls. These range from ensuring the Quality policy of the company is stated and there are sufficient, qualified personnel to carry out this policy; to ensuring that whenever defects occur they are reported and actions introduced to prevent their recurrence. A brief description of the principal requirements of ISO9001 (which contains all the elements of ISO9002 and ISO9003) is given in Appendix 1.

The Quality Standards do not specify any technical requirements for products or services. They only cover the requirements of the management system. They are therefore complementary to any technical standards which may apply to your products and services.

# Implementing your QMS

Most well-run businesses already operate a number of the procedures required by the Quality System Standards as part of their normal day-to-day activities. Once you have determined the appropriate standard, you will need to ensure that your QMS conforms to it. One of the most time consuming activities when seeking approval for a QMS in a well-organised company is preparing documentation to describe the business processes, and then controlling and amending the documents as the business evolves. It is important to try and make your QMS reflect existing processes, rather than change what is done to conform to a pre-determined system. This is one of the principal reasons for involving the whole company in documenting and implementing your QMS. A

| Title of clause | Clause number | | |
| --- | --- | --- | --- |
| | ISO9001 Design, production, installation and servicing | ISO9002 Production and installation | ISO9003 Final inspection and test |
| Management responsibility | 4.1 | 4.1 | 4.1 |
| Quality system | 4.2 | 4.2 | 4.2 |
| Contract review | 4.3 | 4.3 | – |
| Design control | 4.4 | – | – |
| Document and data control | 4.5 | 4.5 | 4.5 |
| Purchasing | 4.6 | 4.6 | – |
| Control of customer-supplied product | 4.7 | 4.7 | – |
| Product identification and traceability | 4.8 | 4.8 | 4.8 |
| Process control | 4.9 | 4.9 | – |
| Inspection and testing | 4.10 | 4.10 | 4.10 |
| Control of inspection, measuring and test equipment | 4.11 | 4.11 | 4.11 |
| Inspection and test status | 4.12 | 4.12 | 4.12 |
| Control of non-conforming product | 4.13 | 4.13 | 4.13 |
| Corrective and preventive action | 4.14 | 4.14 | – |
| Handling, storage, packaging, preservation and delivery | 4.15 | 4.15 | 4.15 |
| Control of quality records | 4.16 | 4.16 | 4.16 |
| Internal Quality audits | 4.17 | 4.17 | – |
| Training | 4.18 | 4.18 | 4.18 |
| Servicing | 4.19 | 4.19 | – |
| Statistical techniques | 4.20 | 4.20 | 4.20 |

**Fig. 1.1 Comparison of the requirements of the ISO9000 series series of standards**

13

consultant can play an important role in training and interpreting the standards for you. But beware the 'off-the-shelf' QMS, whether produced internally or by a consultant! These may act as a strait-jacket and will generally fail in the longer term.

The key requirements for an effective QMS are:

(i)   commitment from senior management;

(ii)  a manager responsible for the integrity of the QMS with sufficient resources to support him;

(iii) documented procedures and records; and

(iv)  periodic, rigorous review of the system.

These issues should be clearly addressed in the documentation which describes your policy for Quality.

# 2

# Quality management improves performance

■ Quality management will help you succeed

■ What do your customers want?

■ Meeting customer requirements

■ The process model

■ Understanding processes

■ Controlling processes

## Quality management will help you succeed

Successful businesses understand their marketplace and their customers. They thrive because they are able to provide products or services which solve their customers' needs at a profit. Other organisations, such as the National Health Service, are successful when they supply the maximum level of service for a given fixed cost. A successful business must be organised so it can identify and meet the needs of its customers at minimum cost. A successful business is therefore an efficient business in which every process is directed towards meeting the requirements of its customers first time every time.

This is exactly what an effective Quality Management System (QMS) seeks to do.

In order to maximise the benefits you receive from your QMS, it is likely that you will want to obtain external recognition for your efforts. Your QMS should therefore be designed to meet the requirements of ISO9000. However, an effective Quality Management System is more than just meeting the requirements of ISO9000. Its principal objective is to ensure that you identify your customers and their requirements, and that you consistently meet those requirements at minimum overall cost. The aims of an effective Quality Management System are the same as those of a successful business. Implementing an effective QMS can make an important contribution to profitability and success.

Unfortunately, many organisations implement a QMS merely to gain ISO9000 registration. As a result, they do not gain any of the real benefits of an effective QMS. They merely address the ISO9000 requirements as a set of additional hurdles for their business. This type of system frequently becomes a bureaucracy which generates piles of paperwork with little to contribute to the business. In the long term, this type of system may well develop into a liability. You will gain infinitely more if you build the requirements of ISO9000 into the very fabric of your business, to help define and control key processes.

Understanding your business and defining an appropriate QMS does take time and effort. Management must be committed to the process and be involved at every step. They must also ensure adequate resources are allocated to the process. However, understanding your business and developing a Quality Management System to document and control it can significantly improve performance. You need to decide if you are prepared to invest to improve!

Ensuring you meet all the requirements of your customers means that you must understand your customers and their requirements and understand and control the processes within your business which contribute to meeting the requirements of your customers.

ISO9000 strictly only requires you to control the activities which have a direct impact on your ability to deliver conforming goods and services to external customers. This does nothing to help you meet the, often unstated, 'implied' requirements of your customers. In times of stiff competition it is often your ability to meet these 'implied' customer requirements that ensures business success. The choice about how broadly you apply your Quality Management System is a commercial decision. ISO9000 only really describes the minimum requirement.

## What do your customers want?

Most organisations are aware of their principal customers and the people within that organisation who are the focal point for component, material, service and product purchases. But these are not the only people within your customer's organisation who might have a view on your performance. Do you know who else within your customers' organisation might assess your performance against their requirements?

Your customer's operations team might monitor the quality of the goods you supply to them, or the response times for service call-outs. If they are dissatisfied with your performance they are likely to look for another supplier. Their goods receiving department may have requirements about when and how goods should be delivered. Their finance department will have requirements concerning the address and content of your invoice. Liaison with their marketing team might enable you to co-operate in the design of new products to your mutual advantage.

Each of these customers may influence the decision to purchase goods or services from you. It is important to understand the requirements of all the groups within your customer's organisation which influence their purchasing decision. Only then will you be able to try and satisfy their requirements.

17

Customer requirements may be divided into two key categories:

(1) 'Defined' requirements are those which must be met by the delivered product or service. They are often specified in the contract and may include some, or all, of the following:

    (i) size, weight, colour, texture and taste;

    (ii) functions, reliability, response times and facilities required;

    (iii) packaging, labelling, delivery times and methods;

    (iv) cost and payment arrangements;

    (v) customer support required; and

    (vi) response times to failures.

These are the basic requirements for each product or service. They are the minimum customer requirements which must be met if a product or service is to be considered satisfactory.

(2) 'Implied' requirements are unstated, but create an overall perception of your business in the eyes of your customers. It's the little things that show you really care for your customers. And the effort you take will generally be well received.

Examples of factors which may influence the impression you give your customers may include:

- *Quotations and order entry*: Are quotations professionally presented and sent out promptly? Are prices and delivery dates firm for a reasonable period of time? When orders are taken do you ensure you record specific delivery requirements (such as day and time of delivery)? Do you ensure customers are always kept informed and offered alternatives if agreed delivery dates cannot be met?

- *Invoicing*: Are invoices accurate and sent out promptly? Do you always follow specific customer instructions for the address and contents? Do you send regular statements of account?

- *Telephone answering*: How easy is it to get through to the person you want to speak to? Are calls answered courteously and promptly? Do receptionists know where people are? Are messages taken reliably? If the contact is not available, will someone else take 'ownership' of the problem? Is the switchboard manned at all 'reasonable' times including lunchtimes and after office hours?

- *Reception area*: Does the reception area give the impression you would like to give? Are these areas attractive and comfortable? Are customers made to feel welcome? Are they offered coffee and a reasonable selection of reading? Is there a visitors' board?

- *Correspondence*: Does all correspondence create a professional image? Is there a standard layout? Are letters well written and free from errors and corrections? Are all letters acknowledged and replied to promptly? Are customers kept informed of the reasons for, and the likely duration of, any delay?

- *Meetings*: Do your employees turn up for meetings on time? Are they adequately prepared for the meeting? Do they have all the equipment and information required? If your people are chairing the meeting, is there an agenda? Do the meetings run to schedule?

- *Systems reliability*: Many organisations have computer systems which dictate the way some activities are performed. Are these systems reliable such that customer orders can be taken and queries answered? It is very frustrating for a customer to be told that their question cannot be answered at the moment because 'the system is down'!

These features of customer service are often overlooked, but can make a lasting impression. Every individual who contacts customers creates an impression of your company. It is important that a professional impression is given at every level, in every activity. Your business has to

18

demonstrate it is committed to Quality and to customer satisfaction. Everyone is a potential future customer and should be treated as such.

Having developed an understanding of your customers and their real requirements, you need to ensure you meet them at minimum cost to the business. But how can you plan to meet the requirements of your external customers?

## Meeting customer requirements

When you action an order from an external customer you go through the following steps:

(i)    you agree with the customer the specification for the product or service they require;

(ii)   you ensure you have the necessary raw materials to produce what is wanted. This material may include components, materials, products, services or information. These are the inputs to the process which you will process to produce the required output;

(iii)  you gather together the necessary tools to enable you to produce the required output. This may include skills and knowledge, plant and equipment, consumables, procedures, information and instructions. How well you manage these 'control parameters' will determine whether you are successful in producing the required output; and

(iv)   you produce what is required and deliver it to your customer.

## The process model

This process of adding value to inputs to produce the output required by your customer is illustrated in the process model (Fig 2.1).

This basic picture is complicated by the fact that external customer requirements can only be met by the correct functioning of internal processes. A number of processes may work together to meet the external customer requirements.

This may give rise to a number of often complex internal supplier-customer chains. You will only satisfy the requirements of your customer at minimum cost if you control these processes so their output is

19

20

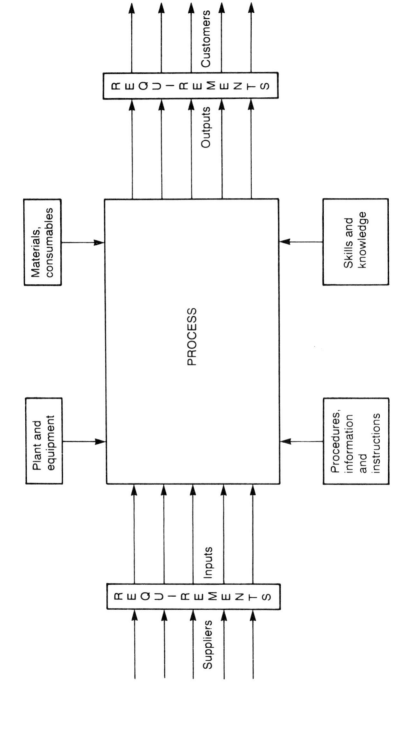

**Fig. 2.1 The process model**

produced right first time. This can only be achieved if customer requirements are identified and met at each stage in the chain. For this purpose:

- a supplier is anyone who supplies input to a process
- a customer is anyone who receives output from a process. Each person is a customer of the previous process in the chain and a supplier to the next process.

Understanding your business as a series of interacting processes and then determining how controlling each process is the most important step towards implementing an effective Quality Management System. To achieve this requires:

(i)   an understanding of the process model and its application to your business;

(ii)  an understanding of what causes variability in a process. Controlling this variability is the key to producing conforming output;

(iii) an understanding of how to identify, understand and control your business processes; and

(iv)  documentation of the processes and controls within your business. This enables operators to ensure processes are effectively controlled.

We will look at these points in the rest of this chapter.

## WHAT IS A PROCESS?

A process is any activity which takes an input and transforms it into an output. Figure 2.1 illustrates the basic characteristics of a typical process. Any process can be described in this way.

Let's look at the supplier/customer relationships which arise in the case of a meeting between a salesman and a customer to discuss the services a business can provide. Here, the customer requires a formal proposal within 48 hours so he can award the contract. The activities associated with producing the output (in this case the proposal document) are illustrated in Fig 2.2(a). Fig 2.2(b) shows similar activities in a professional firm where the client requires advice within 48 hours.

Even an apparently simple process can require a number of inputs to enable it to produce the correct output. Consider just one part of the overall process described above, simply typing the proposal document.

21

| Activity | Comments | Common failures |
|---|---|---|
| 1. Meeting the customer | *1. The customer briefs the salesman*<br><br>(a) Here, the salesman relies on the information supplied by his external customer. | (i) Not all the requirements are identified. |
| 2. Salesman prepares proposal in manuscript or by dictation<br><br>3. The secretary types the draft proposal | *2/3. The salesman gives a draft proposal to his secretary*<br><br>(a) At this point the salesman is the supplier to his secretary. The secretary should insist on the salesman providing enough information to enable the process to be completed right first time. | (i) The salesman's writing might be illegible or his voice indistinct.<br>(ii) The salesman might not specify a timescale for completing the typing.<br>(iii) The secretary might be overloaded and unable to achieve the deadline.<br>(iv) The salesman might not deliver the draft in time for it to be typed. |
| 4. The secretary passes the draft proposal to the salesman for review<br><br>5. The salesman reviews the draft proposal and signs it | *4/5. The secretary returns the draft proposal to the salesman*<br><br>(a) Now the secretary is the supplier to the salesman.<br>(b) Any deficiencies in the information given to the secretary will show up at this point.<br>(c) The action of reviewing a draft proposal is an appraisal activity. If the salesman got it right when he drafted the proposal, and the secretary typed it correctly, it could be run off in final in the first instance. | (i) Typing might be delayed by interruptions.<br>(ii) The wrong format might be used for the proposal.<br>(iii) No spelling checks might be operated.<br>(iv) Typing may be inaccurate.<br>(v) For important documents it might be acceptable to run off a draft at this stage. Routine documents should be run off in final. |
| 6. The salesman sends the draft proposal to the customer | *6. The salesman sends the draft proposal to the customer*<br><br>(a) The customer requires the proposal on his desk within 48 hours of the meeting. | (i) Beware the internal mail system for urgent post. |

**Fig. 2.2(a) Illustration of supplier/customer relationships in a sales organisation**

| Activity | Comments | Common failures |
|---|---|---|
| Meeting the client. The Client aks for advice on a problem | *The client briefs the partner*<br><br>Here, the partner is the salesman. He relies on the information supplied by his client. | Not all the requirements are identified. |
| Partner briefs manager | *Internal briefings*<br><br>Here the partner and manager are the suppliers. The recipient should ensure they have enough information to complete the job properly first time. | Inadequate briefings are common. You must ask for what you want. If you do not then you are unlikely to get it. Your briefing should specify objectives which are:<br><br>● Measurable<br>● Achievable<br>● Specific.<br>● Trackable |
| Manager briefs his staff | | |
| Staff member prepares draft answer | *The staff member prepares the draft answer*<br><br>Deficient briefings will show up at this point. | ● Wrong technical procedures used<br>● Wrong format for letter<br>● Spelling not checked<br>● Not back on time<br>● Wrong address |
| The secretary types the draft answer | | Any number of things could go wrong. It's your job to ensure they do not. |
| The secretary passes the draft answer to the member of staff for review | *The review process*<br><br>Now the staff member is the supplier to the manager. The action of reviewing a draft answer is an appraisal activity. If the member of staff got it right when they drafted the reply, and the secretary typed it correctly, it could be run off in final in the first instance. | For important documents it might be acceptable to run off a draft at this stage. Routine documents should be run off in final. |
| The member of staff reviews the draft answer and gives it to their manager | | |
| The manager reviews the draft answer and gives it to their partner | | |
| The partner reviews the draft answer, signs it and sends it to the client | *The partner sends the answer to the client*<br><br>The client requires the answer on his desk within 48 hours of the meeting. | Partners should ensure they minimise risk and adopt a scientific approach to reviewing. Ensure procedures have been followed and check significant issues. The detailed review should be done by the manager. |

23

**Fig. 2.2(b) Illustration of supplier/customer relationships in a professional firm**

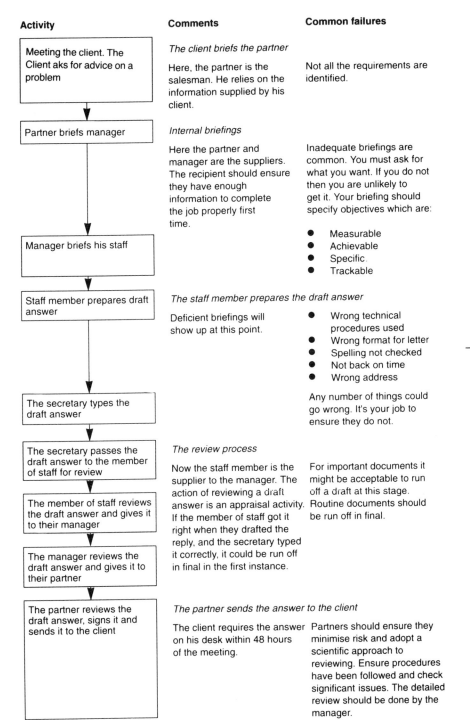

The process diagram for this is illustrated in Fig 2.3. Here, the key process requirements are:

- the proposal dictated by the salesman (the direct inputs)
- equipment (in this case a word processor and photocopier)
- raw materials (paper and toner)
- knowledge of how the equipment works
- procedures or instructions on how the proposal should be set out
- a dictionary or spell check facility to eliminate spelling errors
- experience or training to type
- information on when the proposal is required.

A number of requirements must be satisfied if the process is to be carried out right first time. Establishing the external customer's requirements is an essential first step. This establishes the process requirements. For example, if the customer did not require the proposal until a week after the meeting, then the secretary would not need the dictated draft proposal within 24 hours of the meeting.

Understanding processes; how they are linked together in a supplier/customer chain; and the requirements for each process in the chain is essential if you are to control your business. This enables you to focus on increasing customer satisfaction and reducing the costs of non-conformance. To meet customer requirements at minimum depends on three factors:

(i) ensure customer requirements are understood and defined;

(ii) ensure internal processes which enable you to meet customer requirements are defined; and

(iii) ensure all processes are controlled to ensure they produce conforming output.

## PROCESS VARIABILITY – THE CAUSE OF NON-CONFORMING OUTPUT

However output is characterised (by physical dimensions, number produced per hour, timekeeping of a transport system or the cleanliness of a hotel room) there will be some variation in output. 'Innate' variability will be present in any process. It arises as a result of the variability which exists in each of the control parameters. When a process is running 'in control' the variability of control parameters is within known limits and

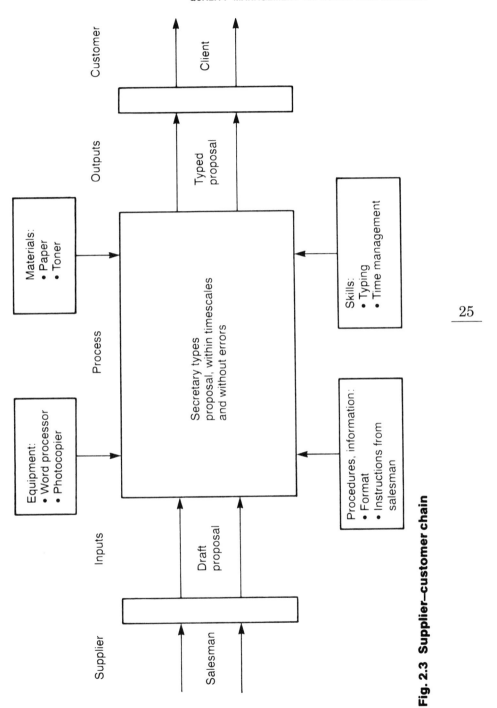

**Fig. 2.3 Supplier–customer chain**

25

the output will vary within definable limits. Your task as a manager is to ensure processes are controlled so they produce outputs which vary between acceptable limits and so customer requirements are met.

Take an example. You run a local bus service and your stated goal is to ensure the arrival of every bus within one minute of its scheduled time. In this way you hope to maximise customer satisfaction and usage. Under normal circumstances the traffic and road conditions mean buses arrive within the defined time. Unfortunately when a new traffic system is introduced at a major set of traffic lights, it causes a delay to your buses of between zero and seven minutes. No matter what you do, that level of variability makes it impossible for your buses to reach the following stops consistently within one minute of the scheduled time. In this case it is necessary either to change the process, perhaps by seeking another route, or to change the process requirements to match the process capability.

As the process stands, it is incapable of meeting your defined output requirement, because you cannot adequately control one of the process control parameters. You need to identify the factors preventing you from producing a conforming service:

26

- the new traffic lights
- a new driver who doesn't know the route
- a faulty bus that cannot accelerate and keep up with the traffic.

There could be many reasons why a process does not produce conforming output. Once you have identified the reasons, you can introduce corrective actions (a new route, driver training, regular servicing of the bus). These steps might mean you are able to meet your requirements. If these measures do not solve the problem then you must renegotiate the output requirements. A commitment to Quality means a commitment to ensure that output requirements are met. It is not acceptable to ignore instances of non-conformance. They must be investigated and result in either the process or the requirements being formally amended.

Understanding how processes operate will enable you to ensure they are capable of meeting the output requirements, notwithstanding the innate variability within a process. Once you have established that a process is capable of meeting the output requirements, then you will know that instances of non-conforming output must be caused by a change either in the inputs to the process or to the control parameters. Understanding process control parameters should enable you to instigate a logical investigation should a problem be identified with the output. You will then be able to effect corrective actions to ensure output conforms to customer requirements.

## IDENTIFYING PROCESSES

Before attempting to control processes, you need to understand their inputs, their customers and how they work. An important first step is to flow chart the processes within your business showing the outputs and how they link together.

Having identified the 'macro processes' in your business you should break these down to identify discrete processes which you can control. The initial flow chart for a manufacturing facility might include a process called 'storage'. This receives inputs from external suppliers and supplies outputs to the production area.

When broken down further the 'storage' process might be described as a series of 'micro' processes:

27

- receiving process – examine, record, identify, pack
- stores allocation – allocate space, mark product, move stock to storage location, update records
- stores issue – receive demand, check authorisation, identify stock, move stock, obtain receipt, update record
- inventory control – analyse stores movements, check numbers and condition, loss reconciliation.

Each of these processes includes a number of separate activities. Having identified the processes and how they link together to meet the requirements of your customers, you need to understand how each process operates so you can control it.

# Understanding processes

Understanding processes will enable you to determine how to control them to reduce variability and improve your ability to meet customer requirements first time, every time. All processes can be described in terms of what they are designed to achieve, together with the arrangements made to ensure that this happens.

## REQUIREMENTS ANALYSIS

The purpose of any process is to produce output to meet a customer requirement. This will only happen if the process owner and the process customer agree on the customer's requirements and how conformance to these requirements can be measured. This is requirements analysis. The process requirements should only be defined after the process owner and the customer have negotiated and agreed what is required.

For most processes, the customer will be an internal customer.

If you conduct this analysis you will probably find significant differences between what is currently produced and what the process customer really wants and needs. In many cases you will find that customers have suffered in silence for a long time and may have developed their own solutions to the problem of not receiving output as they would like it! You will, therefore, need to be sensitive about how you initiate this process. Bear in mind also that process requirements may well change as business needs change.

Once the output requirements have been agreed the process owner can then define the specific tasks which have to be carried out to meet these output requirements.

## SYSTEM ANALYSIS

System analysis is used to determine how each process is designed to operate and the parameters which control it. The control elements, which are shown in Fig 2.4, fall into the following categories:

*Facilities* – the resources and equipment required to operate the process.

*Materials* – any consumables required in order to operate the process.

*People* – a definition of necessary training, experience and personal characteristics important in controlling the process.

*Standards* – a definition of the process requirements in terms of process specifications, operating instructions and procedures.

The objective is to obtain a full definition of how the process is designed to operate. If process owners know what their customers want and understand how to control their processes, then they will be able to meet their customers' requirements at minimum cost.

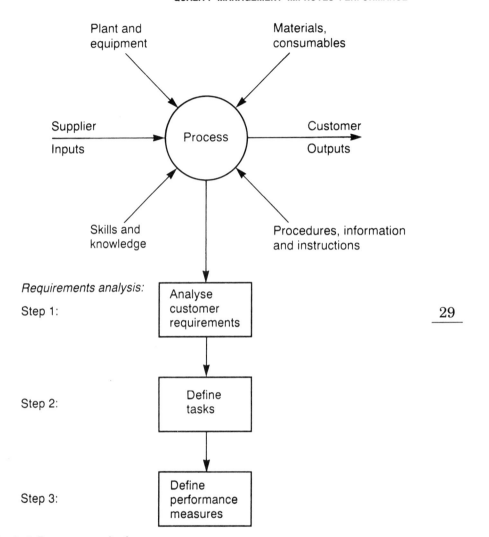

Fig. 2.4  Process analysis

# Controlling processes

Many businesses start to define their Quality Management System on the basis of analysing all the individual *tasks* within the business. This fails to recognise the fundamental purpose of a QMS: that is to satisfy customer requirements. It is quite likely that many of the tasks businesses undertake do not satisfy the requirements of their customers.

You will only be able to define an effective QMS if you identify the requirements of your customers and the processes you will operate to meet those requirements. Then you can start to consider the individual tasks which need to be done to support those processes.

Documenting processes ensures you focus on customer requirements and then define what you need to do to meet those requirements first time every time. Take, for example, the production of monthly management reports on business performance. Documenting the existing tasks of gathering, processing and analysing data will merely record the current activity of producing a 45-page report each month. It, however, does little to address the real customer requirement of the process which is 'The production of management information', not the production each month of a 45-page report! It is quite likely that the existing management report does not meet the needs of management. In this case managers and the finance team should define what is wanted. The finance team can then define the processes and process controls needed to ensure the right information is available, in the right format, to the right people at the right time.

Implementation of a Quality Management System which starts by understanding and controlling business processes will have a significant impact on improving your ability to manage your business, increase customer satisfaction and increase profitability. Starting by defining the tasks you already do will merely fossilise what may in some cases be bad practice.

In a successful business all processes need to work in harmony to meet the requirements of external customers. Processes also need to be performed right first time in order to maximise profitability. Using the process model as a basis for the QMS has three key advantages:

(i)   it ensures the QMS recognises the fundamental processes within the business rather than a series of tasks;

(ii)  by controlling these processes, the QMS will enable you to meet customer requirements at minimum cost; and

(iii) documenting processes, rather than individual tasks, minimises the number of documents within the QMS. This helps ensure the system is 'user friendly' and will be a real basis for managing the business.

The process model enables management to control key business processes. They do not have to define the individual tasks of every person in the organisation, provided they are satisfied that processes are controlled so customer needs are met. This should establish a fertile environment dedicated to satisfying the requirements of customers and enabling employees to have some control over their own working pattern. In this way the control mechanisms are defined, the outcome of each process is generally as expected, individuals responsible for making the whole thing work have personal involvement, and the definition and documentation task is not overly burdensome.

31

# Planning for registration

- **The approval bodies**
- **The approval process**
- **Costs and timescales**
- **Summary**

## The approval bodies

The credibility of any certification process depends on two key points:

(i)   acceptance of the Standard itself; and

(ii)  acceptance of the certification process and the certification bodies as competent, fair and professional.

The British Standards Institute (BSI) is responsible for the issue and control of BS EN ISO9000 in the UK. The BSI is also one of the organisations which can carry out assessments and award ISO9000 certification. There are in fact more than 30 accredited certification bodies in the UK. These are independent assessment organisations and include, for example, the BSI, Lloyds Register, and Yarsley. A selected list of the accredited certification bodies is set out in Appendix 11.

In 1982, the Government signalled its support for BS5750 certification (now ISO9000) in a White Paper entititled 'Standards, Quality and International Competitiveness'. This recognised that assessment and certification of supplier quality systems was rapidly replacing inspection as a means of gaining assurance of the quality of supplies. It gave responsibility for administering and publicising the national certification process to the Department of Trade and Industry (DTI). It also recognised the demand for a system to ensure the competence and integrity of the bodies carrying out certification. It responded to this demand by establishing a scheme to ensure a professionally run certification process.

The National Accreditation Council for Certification Bodies (NACCB) was set up to monitor and administer the certification process on behalf of the Secretary of State for Trade and Industry. The NACCB includes representatives from industry, trade unions, the public utilities and local government. There is also one member who represents all the certification bodies. The NACCB manages and directs the UK accreditation and certification system. Its principal responsibilities include:

- assessing and recommending certification bodies for accreditation to the Secretary of State for Trade and Industry
- monitoring the performance of certification bodies
- ensuring the certification bodies have adequate systems and technical skills to carry out competent assessments
- addressing issues which customers cannot resolve with their certification body.

## SECOND- OR THIRD-PARTY ASSESSMENT?

It is not always necessary to seek certification of your Quality Management System from one of the accredited independent assessing bodies. In some cases conformance to the standard may be assessed by the customer placing the contract. This is known as second-party assessment. Here the customer assesses your Quality Management System (QMS) solely for its suitability to fulfil the requirements of their contract. They may carry out their assessment against the requirements of ISO9000 but they cannot award a certificate of registration to ISO9000.

Most businesses opt for an independent assessment by an approved accredited body. This is known as third-party assessment. In this case a successful assessment may lead to ISO9000 registration.

## WHICH CERTIFICATION BODY SHOULD YOU USE?

The certification body you choose will be responsible for assessing your Quality Management System against the requirements of ISO9000 and awarding registration. It is important to select your assessing body carefully as there are differences between them. There are four key criteria to use when selecting the appropriate certification body for your business:

(i)  *Competency* – the need to have adequate technical ability limits the type of organisation/industry for which a certification body is approved to carry out assessments and award certificates. Each certification body is therefore limited to carrying out assessments for a specified range of industries.

Only an accredited body whose scope of approval covers your business activities is accredited to award registration to ISO9000 for your organisation. It is important to ensure the body you select is accredited and that the scope of its accreditation covers your business activities. Many organisations are able to carry out an assessment against ISO9000, but only an appropriate accredited body can award registration which is universally recognised.

(ii) *Experience* – even though a certification body may be accredited to certify your type of business, their experience in actually carrying out assessments may be limited. A body with extensive experience may better understand your business and how an effective QMS should operate. They may also be able to carry out the assessment more quickly than an inexperienced team, so saving you money!

35

(iii) *Costs and timescales* – each certification body will provide a quotation for carrying out your assessment based on their estimate of how long it will take. There are no standard charges so you should compare costs from two or three bodies. The assessment bodies will also quote different lead times before they are able to carry out your assessment. Again, shop around and select the body which meets your needs.

(iv) *Compatibility* – it is important that you feel comfortable with your assessing body. Talk to a number of bodies. Assess their style, their responsiveness and their openness, and select a body which suits your needs.

When dealing with the certification body, remember that they are assessing your System at your request – *they are your supplier.*

# The approval process

Any company may apply to an accredited body for assessment and approval. Figure 3.1 describes a typical assessment process from initial selection of the certification body through to registration. The following are the key stages in the process:

(i) Define the activities for which you are seeking registration to ISO9000. This may be your whole organisation or just part of it. If you have a number of sites or offices, you may choose to seek approval for only one or some of them. If you carry out a wide range of activities, you may choose only to seek registration for part of the business.

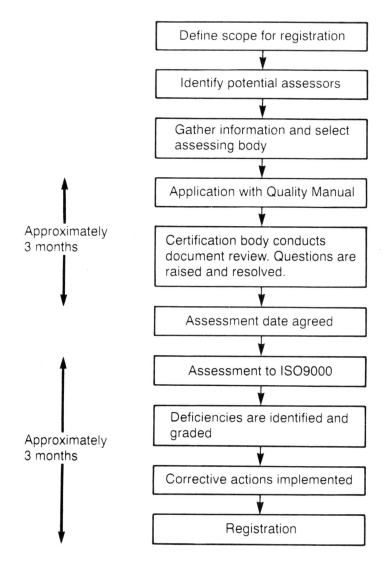

**Fig. 3.1 The registration process**

For example, an accountancy firm might choose to seek registration for its management consultancy, training, tax or auditing services; or all of them. A law firm might choose to seek registration only for its conveyancing activity. A health authority might choose only to seek registration for their ambulance service. Defining the scope for registration must be thought through carefully since it influences:

- the cost and complexity of registration
- the range of approval bodies which can carry out the assessment
- the services for which you will later be able to claim registration.

(ii) Identify the certification bodies whose scope cover the activities for which you are seeking approval. For some activities, such as legal or accounting services, there may be relatively few certification bodies. In other industry sectors the choice will be much wider.

(iii) Obtain quotes from two or three bodies for the costs and timescales involved in the assessment process. Talk to other registered companies about their experiences. Talk to the certification bodies to gauge their approach and professionalism. Having gathered this basic data, you will be in a position to make a decision on the appropriate certification body for your organisation.

37

(iv) Make an application to your selected certification body. At this stage, if you haven't already done so, you will be asked to complete an application form defining the size of your organisation and the scope of the activities for which you are seeking registration. The certification body will use this information for a number of purposes:

- verifying they are approved to carry out the assessment
- determining the size of the assessing team required. This will determine the final cost of the assessment
- deciding whether any specific skills will be required on the team
- determining what additional information they require from you.

(v) At this stage the assessing body will request some supporting documentation to enable them to determine how well your QMS, as documented, conforms to the requirements of ISO9000. They will usually ask you to send them a copy of your Quality Manual (your policy document), your organisation structure and responsibilities (organisation charts and job descriptions for key senior managers will usually suffice here), and a number of key procedures. The best way to handle this stage of the assessment is just to provide what the certification body requests.

The certification body will review this documentation against the requirements of ISO9000 and raise any questions they feel are necessary. This is an important stage in the certification process. Unless the certification body is reasonably satisfied with your QMS as it is documented, they will not waste their time or your money carrying out a physical audit to confirm that the QMS is actually being followed.

(vi) Having satisfied themselves that your QMS, as documented, meets the requirements of ISO9000, the certification body will agree an assessment date. This is when they will visit your company to audit your QMS. This date may generally be changed if you decide it is no longer convenient. You are the customer.

During the audit, the assessment team will look for evidence that:

- the QMS is effective and is being applied

- the QMS is regularly reviewed to ensure it is effective and continues to meet the requirements of ISO9000 and your customers

- there is understanding and commitment to the QMS at all levels in the organisation.

The assessment team will seek objective evidence of the effectiveness of the QMS and that it is being applied. They have two principal sources for this evidence:

- talking to individuals to verify their understanding of the QMS and conformance to it

- looking at the records to determine whether or not the QMS has been followed. If the QMS is being operated at present and has a history of being followed, this increases confidence that it will continue to be followed.

(vii) At the end of the assessment, a final meeting will be held to discuss the results. For larger audits there may be a number of intermediate reviews to keep you informed of findings. At these meetings audit deficiencies will be raised and the company will be asked for comments. At the final meeting you will be informed of the result of the audit. There are three possible outcomes:

- the QMS has been approved and registration recommended. In this case either no deficiencies will have been found, or the deficiencies are so minor that they can be dealt with at the next routine surveillance visit

- a number of more significant deficiencies have been found. Once these have been addressed the organisation will be registered. This is the most frequent outcome for organisations which have invested time and effort to develop their QMS.

■ a number of major deficiencies have been identified which require significant changes to the QMS. Here the organisation will have failed the audit and a complete re-assessment will be required once the deficiencies have been cleared.

## POST REGISTRATION

Once an organisation has been registered, it is entitled to the following:

(i)    a certificate confirming registration;

(ii)   listing in the DTI QA Register. This is a list of all registered organisations. It is published annually, with intermediate updates, and is used extensively by purchasing organisations; and

(iii)  freedom to use the registered company logo on publicity material and stationery. The logo may not be used on product since it is a management system approval and not a product approval.

39

The initial registration is valid for three years. During the registration period, the certification body has to gain assurance that the QMS continues to be followed and is effective. This is achieved by a number of routine surveillance visits during the registration period to audit specific aspects of the QMS. The dates for the surveillance visits are agreed in advance.

During these visits the external assessors look particularly on the system for internal audits. Effective internal audits are a powerful indicator of management commitment to ensure their Quality Management System continues to be effective and followed. It is important to be able to demonstrate that your QMS continues to conform to the requirements of ISO9000.

After three years, the certification body will normally carry out a complete re-assessment of your QMS.

# Costs and timescales

Every organisation is unique in terms of its size, complexity, conformance of the current system to the requirements of ISO9000, and the level of skill/resource available to implement a QMS. Consequently it is impossible to estimate costs and timescales for the whole registration process. The majority of organisations apply for registration once their QMS is virtually complete. In this case, the following broad timescales generally apply. It commonly takes about three months for the assessing body to complete its desktop review of the QMS. This allows time for questions to be asked and answered, but assumes the QMS broadly conforms to the requirements of ISO9000 and no major re-writing is required. It generally takes about three months from assessment before registration is complete, assuming only a small number of minor deficiencies are found at assessment.

Costs are basically incurred at four stages during registration:

(i)   initial application;

(ii)  initial assessment;

(iii) regular surveillance visits during the registration period; and

(iv)  re-assessment after three years.

All costs for the assessment process (including the subsequent surveillance visits) have to be met by the organisation applying for registration. These costs may vary enormously. They depend on the number of man-days involved in assessing the organisation. The level of cost generally depends on three factors:

(i)   the size of the organisation, measured by the number of employees. The more employees, the higher the cost;

(ii)  the complexity of the activities being carried out. Generally the costs of registration under ISO9001 are greater than for ISO9002 or ISO9003 because more processes are involved; and

(iii) the number of sites for which the organisation requires registration. This probably has the greatest influence on cost. If the sites all carry out broadly similar activities and follow the same systems, then the certification body may audit a small sample number of sites to verify conformance. If multiple sites all carry out different activities then the certification body may wish to carry out an assessment at each site. One way to minimise costs is to apply for company-wide approval which covers a wide variety of activities carried out on multiple sites under a common registration. If you choose to go down this route you would need to discuss the approach in considerable detail with the certification body concerned.

# Summary of the approval process

The following is a summary of the basic approval process:

(i)   recognised certification can only be carried out by an NACCB accredited body;

(ii)  the initial registration is generally valid for three years;

(iii) routine surveillance audits are carried out regularly;

(iv)  re-assessment is normally carried out after three years;

(v)   all costs are borne by the organisation requesting registration;

(vi)  the certification body is *your supplier*.

## DEVELOPING A PLAN TO ACHIEVE REGISTRATION

A Quality Management System has two interrelated requirements:

- it must satisfy the needs and expectations of your external customers
- it must satisfy the needs and interests of your company and employees.

41

A QMS which achieves these objectives will play a key role in the overall management of your business. An effective Quality Management System is designed to improve your control over your business.

Successful implementation and registration will only be achieved if your QMS is wanted, understood, planned and managed. The only people who can make this commitment are senior management. Management commitment is key to ensuring a successful QMS.

However, the QMS must also be understood and implemented throughout the organisation. This will only happen if it involves all your employees.

# 4

# Establishing the framework for an effective Quality Management System

- The role of senior management: leadership by example
- Securing the support of your employees
- The role of the management representative
- Ensuring your QMS continues to be effective
- Action plan

## The role of senior management: leadership by example

Now we have come to the heart of the matter. What do you, as a senior manager, have to do in order to implement an effective Quality Management System?

You will only achieve an effective Quality Management System if you define your requirements for it. This is your first responsibility.

If you invest time to determine what you want from your management system, and understand what ISO9000 can really deliver, then you will

Note: ISO9001 defines the requirements for management responsibility and the Quality System in paragraphs 4.1 and 4.2.

be able to define a QMS that really works for you. This will give you a significant advantage over other businesses where management simply resign themselves to a QMS that serves no one well.

## WHAT ARE YOUR OBJECTIVES FOR YOUR QUALITY MANAGEMENT SYSTEM?

Clearly you want to organise your business so all the factors (be they technical, administrative or human) affecting the quality of the products or services you produce are under control.

These are the objectives of ISO9000.

The first step is to ensure you have a clear set of objectives for your business. Only then can you start to define your requirements for a QMS. The control environment which you introduce should be designed to reduce, eliminate and prevent quality deficiencies. You will only be able to achieve this if the system is tailored to suit your business.

An effective Quality Management System should be designed to satisfy customer requirements and serve the interests of the company. These objectives can only be achieved if all the resources at your disposal (human, technical and material) are utilised in a planned and efficient way. Your QMS should be designed so it does not overburden you with administration. This aspect is seldom appreciated by those whose experience is of systems that drive the company rather than being driven by the company.

## MANAGEMENT COMMITMENT

Management must define the system which meets the needs of their business. The first step is to secure management commitment to develop and implement an effective QMS. Management must adopt a Quality philosophy which focuses on understanding and meeting customer requirements through preventing errors, not merely fixing them once they have arisen. The commitment required from management to a QMS is absolute if it is to succeed. If management commitment is not absolute then the system will fail. Management must demonstrate their commitment in actions and words. Employees will soon see through new 'fads' that do not have real management support.

Management are responsible for ensuring that the Quality Management System:

- defines the Quality environment (usually known as the Quality Policy) for the business. Management should ensure that their commitment to Quality is understood and followed throughout the organisation
- complies with the requirements of ISO9000
- is operated by all staff
- is fully documented and controlled.

It is common to find a framed notice in the foyer of companies proclaiming a long and complex Quality Policy for all to see. This will usually be signed by the Chief Executive. It is equally common to find that no one can remember or define their Quality Policy.

When developing your Quality Policy remember that it needs to be understood and followed by everyone. They need to know your policy, what it means and how it applies to them. A simple, clear statement is often the best way to achieve this. One of the simplest policies we have seen is:

*We are committed to providing our customers*
*with what they want, every time, at a profit to us.*

It is not a complicated explanation of the company's commitment to excellence, or participative management, or even to ISO9000. It is simply a commitment to give their customers what they want. To deliver the goods and services as they promised, even when it becomes more difficult than they ever thought.

In this case the policy will be understood by everyone: staff, customers and suppliers. The moral is to write the Quality Policy you want your staff to follow and which you are prepared to support without compromise, however tough the going gets. If you and your organisation are not serious about quality, your people and your customers will soon get to know whatever your Quality Policy might state.

The Quality Policy is important. It is a statement of management's Quality objectives for the business; it must be relevant to the supplier and to the needs and expectations of the customer. It must be published throughout the organisation, understood by employees, supported by management and regularly reviewed and maintained. It is one element in the process of demonstrating commitment to Quality. But it is the demonstration by every manager in their day-to-day work that they are *never* prepared to compromise their commitment to Quality that is

45

required by ISO9000 and which will make a QMS succeed. It is important to be able to demonstrate an active management commitment to Quality and also to be able to demonstrate that the senior management commitment is handed down and taken on board by each manager within the organisation. This can be achieved by incorporating into each manager's job description a requirement to implement the organisation's Quality Policy throughout his area of influence.

# Organisation for Quality

If all employees are going to participate in the Quality Management System and ensure that they consistently meet the needs and expectations of customers, they must understand how they fit into the organisation and how they contribute to customer satisfaction. This is achieved by five main means:

- an understanding of the organisation, its goals and a plan for achievement; this is usually achieved by a business plan (see Appendix 5 for a description)

- an understanding of the organisation, how it is structured and how they fit in; this is usually achieved by structured organisational charts (see Appendix 9 for examples)

- an understanding of their role within the organisation; their responsibilities, authorities, key activities and how performance will be measured; this is usually achieved by structured job descriptions (see Appendix 10 for an example)

- regular reviews of their performance so they can discuss their performance and any training and career development required; this is usually achieved by annual appraisals

- an understanding of the processes within the business, how they operate and how they function together to meet customer requirements; this is usually achieved by a Quality Management System documented around key business processes.

These, together with a sincere and well-understood Quality Policy and the demonstrated commitment of management to Quality establish a framework for the development of a successful QMS aimed at meeting customer expectations at minimum cost to the organisation. To put the flesh on the framework and to develop the system then depends on gaining the commitment and support of all employees to contribute and participate in the development.

# The business plan

One of the key management responsibilies in ensuring a successful business, committed to meeting customer needs, is the development of meaningful and effective business plans. An effective business plan describes the aims and goals of the organisation over a time period and the methods, products/services, key activities, organisation and skills necessary to achieve those goals. A good business plan can only come from a detailed understanding of the marketplace, customer needs, how those needs can be met and how the organisation must be geared to respond to those customer needs. An effective business plan is, therefore, a key tool in ensuring the understanding and planning necessary to ensure that the Quality Policy does have some meaning and can be met in practice. Appendix 5 provides an example of a procedure used to describe and control the business planning activity.

47

# Securing the support of your employees

A successful QMS will involve all your employees. Everyone must take ownership for the quality of their work. This will only be achieved if they are involved in developing the system to ensure it meets the objectives of your Quality Policy. This means that:

(i)   all employees need to understand their customers' requirements and the internal processes which enable you to meet those requirements;

(ii)  it will no longer be acceptable to rely on finding and fixing errors. You will will have to focus on preventing errors; and

(iii) individuals should be encouraged to take actions to improve the Quality of their output.

To achieve these objectives will require the commitment of all your employees. It may also require some changes in existing management methods and systems. This may raise difficult questions but these need to be resolved. You are only likely to achieve the required level of personal commitment from your employees if everyone understands the aims and benefits of the QMS and the role they can play. Your employees must:

(i)   believe management wants them to become involved. The attitudes and actions of employees are generally determined by what they believe management wants from them. It is essential that you define clearly and unambiguously what involvement you want from your employees;

(ii) understand what they can contribute. Individuals are generally reluctant to become involved in an activity unless they have been given permission to do so. They need to know their responsibilities, authority to act and the boundaries of their role. This can be achieved by providing them with a well-written job specification. It should not just be a description of the tasks which the employee will be expected to undertake. A properly written job specification can provide the management authority for individual involvement, and resources they have to meet those responsibilities; and

(iii) be provided with the necessary education and training. To achieve the involvement of every employee requires their commitment. Commitment requires understanding. Understanding requires training. Training requires management commitment, planning and time.

Every individual needs to understand the reasons for the QMS, what it means to them and how they are equipped to contribute. The training must be relevant, interesting and enable people to under-stand and participate.

It is important that the whole workforce is included in the training programme. Everyone has their part to play. A receptionist may help to gain or lose a customer as easily as a manager. If a message is not passed on quickly, the customer may choose to look elsewhere for a solution to his needs. Production line staff are likely to know more about the things that are wrong where they work than their managers and supervisors. They have probably been living with the problems and fixing the errors for a number of years. This is equally true for professional firms, manufacturing industries and health service units.

Experience has shown that the most effective approach to training within a company is to cascade the learning process from the manager to the supervisors and then to individual employees. The duration and content of the education programme depends on the individuals being trained. But they should all understand why the QMS is required and their personal involvement in its development and implementation.

## ENSURING OWNERSHIP OF THE QUALITY MANAGEMENT SYSTEM

One difficulty organisations sometimes find when establishing a QMS lies in the unresponsiveness of some employees and managers. In most cases this stems from a belief that 'they' are being told how to do their job by people who have no great claim to excellence themselves.

Clearly, imposing new working practices and systems without consultation is a recipe for disaster at any time. Imposing a QMS without reference to those whose job is affected is worse because they will resent it. This may well ultimately lead to failure of the QMS, higher costs, dissatisfied customers, and disgruntled employees.

The best results will be obtained if employees are involved at all stages in the process. Analysing your business as a series of processes will enable you to determine what goes on, and to identify and manage the control elements that govern the success of your business.

Having identified all the processes in your business, their owners should be involved in documenting them. The first step is to define the technical content, the 'how' and 'what', of each process. These should be defined by people who know what actually happens. In order to ensure consistency you may well wish to establish a standard for preparing documentation. Once the initial data has been recorded, the documents may be polished up by a central team. The owners of the processes should continue to be involved at each stage. They should be closely involved in any discussion about process improvements and changes.

49

This involvement will establish ownership of each process by those who operate it. It will also ensure that details of each process are recorded faithfully. This will establish a base line for improvement throughout the business. This will ensure the system is accepted and operated by all because everyone was involved from the beginning. This is critical to having a cost-effective system for the management of quality.

The individual time commitment to documenting a system in this manner is limited because the workload is shared amongst many employees. This approach does, however, require training:

- management team training
- more extensive training for project leaders
- general awareness training for the workforce.

# The role of the management representative

One commitment that is essential to meet the requirements of ISO9000 is the nomination of a senior manager to be responsible for the continued integrity of the QMS; this role can be combined with other responsibilities. This individual must have the necessary authority to resolve any issues involving the QMS which might arise. It is generally sensible to appoint this individual before starting to implement a QMS. They can then develop their understanding of the application of ISO9000 to your business and can manage the implementation process on behalf of the management team. The management representative has two key roles:

(i)   to ensure that a QMS is developed, implemented and maintained in accordance with ISO9000; and

(ii)  to report on the performance of the QMS to the executive management of the organisation.

A mistake made by many organisations is to task this individual or their team to totally document and implement the QMS. This may initially seem an attractive route to follow, but it may encourage you to focus on the Standard and not on your business needs. This may force your QMS into a mould created by ISO9000. A QMS structured in this way may fail to meet the needs of your business at the moment. It will also probably be difficult to adapt to changing circumstances. Involving everyone in identifying and defining processes might seem time consuming at the outset. However, you will only get real commitment from your staff if they believe the QMS meets their needs. The most effective way of achieving this is to involve your staff in developing the documentation and ensuring they are all collectively responsible for their QMS. The Standard only requires the management representative to ensure a QMS is developed not to actually do the development themselves.

The management representative may be the internal 'expert' on the requirements of ISO9000. They have a responsibility to manage and guide the implementation process but they are not solely responsible for the QMS. Everyone must take ownership for the elements under their control.

The management representative should also monitor the health of the QMS ensuring it continues to meet the needs of the business and of customers and reporting on its effectiveness and any changes required to the executive management of the organisation.

The management representative should not:

(i)  totally write and implement the QMS. This will remove the opportunity for involving individuals in developing (and hence 'owning') the system; or

(ii) assume sole responsibility for the QMS. This responsibility lies with every manager and employee of the company. They cannot delegate responsibility to someone else. Everyone must accept their individual responsibility for ensuring the processes they are responsible for meeting customer requirements at minimum cost to the business.

## USING OUTSIDE CONSULTANTS TO HELP

If you employ individuals with the necessary skills, experience and time to implement your QMS then you will probably not need outside help. If you do not have the necessary expertise in house, you may find it useful to use an experienced project manager from outside. A good consultant will be able to give you an independent view of how to get the best out of a QMS. They will also help you to separate the 'responsibility for quality' from the quality management function. Everyone is responsible for Quality in their work.

An independent consultant could help in the following ways:

- identify the processes involved in producing products and services
- interpret ISO9000 in the context of your business
- liaise between different teams and individuals
- provide project management skills
- assist in the task of producing documentation.

You must, however, retain control of your QMS. The consultant should be driven by you. You should define what you want from your QMS and use the consultant's experience to guide you in doing this. Handing over responsibility for your QMS to a consultant will lead to an ineffective system which does not meet your business needs.

# Ensuring your Quality Management System continues to be effective

Every business changes over time. It is essential that your QMS develops as your business and the marketplace changes. No business is static and no QMS can afford to be static. Senior management should determine key parameters which they will use to monitor the effectiveness of their QMS. This will certainly include internal audit reports; measures of business efficiency (such as process yields, scrap levels, or administration errors); and some measures of customer satisfaction (customer complaints, customer rejects and survey results). By regularly monitoring, reviewing and taking action on these performance measures, management will be able to constantly improve the ability of their QMS to meet customer requirements at minimum cost – the objective of any successful QMS. This enables management to use their QMS as a basis for improving business performance.

52

# Action plan

Implementating an effective QMS and its subsequent registration requires:

- management understanding and commitment
- involvement of all employees
- an action plan to define the steps you will take
- monitoring of progress.

The following steps should be built into your management plan to achieve registration. More detailed plans should be defined for individual activities:

- determine the scope of your business
- ensure senior management understand what is required and are committed to succeed define your Quality Policy
- nominate your management representative and ensure they understand the requirements of ISO9000
- review your current system and determine how well it meets the requirements of ISO9000

- identify what is required to meet the requirements of ISO9000 – a development plan
- ensure individuals understand their role – an education plan
- allocate actions and deadlines to individuals – an implementation plan
- monitor progress – an assessment plan
- apply for registration

## A FINAL NOTE OF CAUTION

Do try to avoid the pitfalls associated with taking an 'easy path' to documenting your QMS. An effective QMS will really help you to do profitable business. A poorly designed system is likely to be ineffective. It will not improve your performance; it is more likely to detract from it.

It is vital that you understand what you want to achieve from your QMS. Then you can ensure you implement a QMS to help you improve business performance.

53

# 5

# The necessary documentation

- **Documentation required**
- **The Quality Manual**
- **Procedures**
- **Work instructions**
- **Controlling the documentation**

## Documentation requirements

A Quality Management System will only be effective if it is documented, understood and followed by all employees. This will only be achieved if it:

- defines procedures for all processes
- is documented and available to all users
- is readily used and understood by all users so everyone knows what is required of them.

The first step is to identify and generate the documents required to fully define the Quality Management System. It is then necessary to control the issuing, changing and withdrawal of these documents so that only properly authorised, current versions are in use.

There are generally three levels of documentation within a Quality Management System. Each level becomes more detailed, more specific and generally applies to fewer people within the organisation. Figure 5.1 illustrates this hierarchy of documents; the so-called pyramid of documentation.

Note: ISO9001 defines the requirements for documents and their controls in paragraphs 4.2 and 4.5.

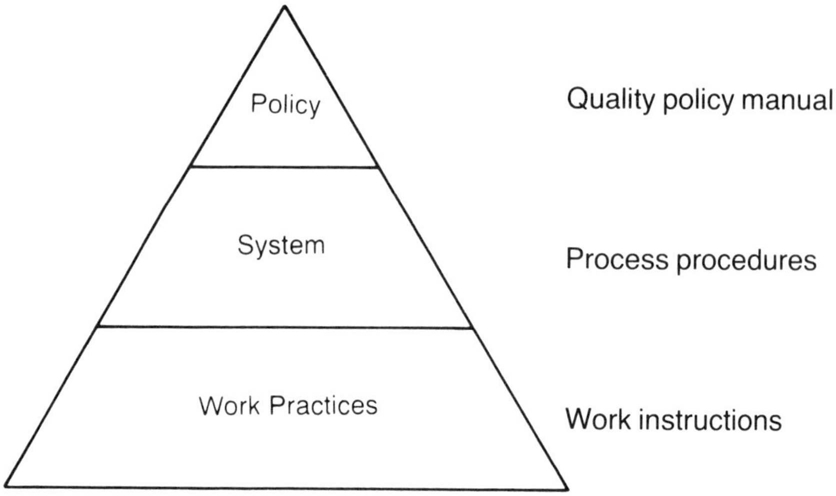

**Fig. 5.1 Hierarchy of documentation**

# The Quality Policy Manual

This is the statement of management policy and objectives on each of the requirements of ISO9000 for your business. It usually begins with a brief description of your business, its history, activities and the scope of the operation to which the QMS applies. The bulk of the manual then defines how each of the ISO9000 requirements is addressed by the Quality Management System. The Quality Manual defines the structure of the QMS; it acts as a 'roadmap' round the system.

The Quality Manual is generally a slim document (often less than 20 pages). It is a policy statement. The remaining documentation within the QMS describes how these objectives are actually met in practice. The Quality Manual is useful for a number of purposes:

(i)   it ensures management understand what commitments the QMS is making on their behalf;

(ii)  it ensures employees understand management policy and use it to guide their activities;

(iii) the assessing bodies use it as a starting point for assessing your QMS. This provides assurance that each element of ISO9000 has been addressed by your QMS, and guides them to areas where further information is required;

(iv) it acts as a roadmap, defining the structure of the Quality Management System;

(v) it provides a basis for assuring customers that your QMS exists. This can be met by supplying a copy of your Quality Manual. This doesn't reveal too much detail about how your business operates; and

(vi) as a marketing tool, it demonstrates the existence of a QMS and your management commitment to Quality.

A typical Quality Manual might include:

- a description of your business, a brief history and current activities
- a definition of the scope of your business and the activities to which the Quality Manual applies
- a description of how your QMS addresses the requirement of each paragraph of ISO9000
- a list of all the procedures which define the QMS.

57

An example of a Quality Manual for an organisation applying for ISO9001 registration is in Appendix 2. (Further guidance on Quality Manuals is given in ISO10013.)

# Procedures

These documents form the bulk of a Quality Management System. They describe how the policy objectives of the Quality Manual are met in practice and how the business processes are controlled.

Procedures describe the controls which exist to ensure all processes operate in such a way that both customer requirements and the requirements of ISO9000 are understood and met. These procedures should describe how the processes work and how they satisfy the requirements of ISO9000. Figure 5.2 illustrates how this works in practice. These procedures generally describe the purpose of the process, how it operates, and the controls which reduce the variability of the process and ensure conforming output. Examples of procedures are included in Appendices 3, 4 and 5.

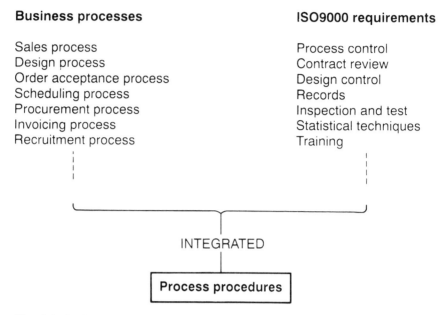

**Business processes**

Sales process
Design process
Order acceptance process
Scheduling process
Procurement process
Invoicing process
Recruitment process

**ISO9000 requirements**

Process control
Contract review
Design control
Records
Inspection and test
Statistical techniques
Training

INTEGRATED

Process procedures

**Fig. 5.2 An integrated Quality Management System**

# Work instructions

These describe how to perform specific activities within a process. For example, a procedure might describe a production testing process. A work instruction might describe how to operate a piece of test equipment. Another procedure might describe the process of carrying out a market survey. A work instruction might describe how to write a questionnaire for a market survey.

ISO9000 only requires work instructions where the absence of such a document would present a hazard to Quality. The number of work instructions required in an organisation depends on the complexity of the operation and the skill, training and experience of the personnel employed. For example, in a catering establishment, the skills and training of a qualified chef would remove the need for detailed work instructions on how to make a cake. However, instructions would be required if the same organisation employed unskilled or inexperienced individuals in this role. In both cases the procedure would document the overall process and its controls. Only the requirements for a detailed work instruction would vary.

Many organisations produce a heavy burden of paperwork because they do not really understand how to develop an effective QMS. They produce a mountain of work instructions, many of which are not really required. When considering the level of work instructions required, a careful balance has to be struck between the volume of documentation required and ensuring that all personnel understand how to undertake activities for which they are responsible. If you document everything, you may produce a great deal of unnecessary paperwork. However, too little documentation can result in uncontrolled processes and non-conforming output. It is a fine balance.

The majority of work involved in implementing your QMS will involve understanding, controlling and documenting your business processes. The remainder of the book takes you through the detailed requirements of ISO9000. It describes how to devise systems to control your business so it:

- meets the needs of your customers
- meets the needs of your business
- enables you to achieve ISO9000 registration.

Having determined and documented your QMS, it is important that these documents are controlled.

However, before you start, it is important that you establish your document control system. There are four main reasons for this:

(i)   it ensures you produce documents so they can be controlled;

(ii)  each document can be authorised and issued as part of your formal system as it is written. Leaving the control system until the end means you have no mechanism for issuing and controlling documents until the documentation task is complete. This will delay implementation and may mean you risk losing momentum in the the registration process;

(iii) it saves the time consuming task of sorting and re-formatting documents once the documentation has been drafted; and

(iv)  it enables you to issue guidelines on the structure and contents of documents. This provides a framework for individuals tasked with producing the documentation.

# Controlling the documentation

Documentation is the key to an effective Quality Management System. It defines the procedures to be operated throughout the business. It is important to ensure these documents are properly authorised and are current so only approved procedures are operated at any time. It is therefore necessary that you control the issuing, changing and withdrawal of Quality documents. The key elements in an effective system of document control are set out in Chapter 12.

---

**CHECKLIST: THE NECESSARY DOCUMENTATION**

1 Have you defined your Quality objectives in a company Quality Policy? How do you ensure this policy is understood and followed by everyone?

2 Have you produced a Quality Manual? Does it address each of the requirements of ISO9000?

3 Have you defined the procedures which you require to control your business? Do these take into account all the ISO9000 requirements?

4 Have you defined the work instructions required?

5 Have you decided how you will control your Quality documents? (see checklist for Chapter 12).

---

# 6

# Giving customers what they want

- ■ **Understanding customer requirements**
- ■ **Planning to meet customer requirements**
- ■ **Agreeing requirements with customers**
- ■ **Checklist**

## Understanding customer requirements

Your objective is to satisfy the requirements of your customers at minimum cost. An effective Quality Management System (QMS) creates an environment in which you can be confident that you will achieve this. Your customers will also be confident that you are able to satisfy their requirements.

The first step is to understand what your customers want. We have looked at how you achieve this in Chapter 2. You then need to ensure you are in a position to respond rapidly to customer requirements as they arise. Then you should enter into a formal agreement to provide what is wanted.

## Planning to meet customer requirements

To ensure you are capable of meeting current and future customer needs, you need to:

- ■ understand the capabilities of your business

Note: ISO9001 defines the requirements for contract review and servicing in paragraphs 4.3 and 4.19.

- regularly review the purpose of your business
- ensure you understand who your customers are
- anticipate future developments in the marketplace
- anticipate future customer requirements.

Taking these steps will ensure you are equipped to respond to changing customer demands. Having identified anticipated customer needs you need to plan your business to ensure these needs can be met.

Planning is not generally popular as an activity. However, a properly developed plan will save time and money because it eliminates the unexpected. Despite this, we never seem to have enough time to do all the planning we need to ensure the work is done correctly and on time! This is usually because we are all too busy doing work over again when it goes wrong, invariably because we failed to plan for success. You have to get over this hurdle if you want to succeed.

Planning is one of the key elements in ensuring you can meet anticipated customer needs and that actual customer requirements are understood and met. So how do we go about planning?

Companies generally adopt one of two types of approach to planning. Some organisations invest time and effort to anticipate future customer requirements and ensure they are equipped to respond (pro-active planning). Others wait until they receive a customer request and then determine how to respond (re-active planning).

Let us consider each of these approaches.

## PRO-ACTIVE PLANNING

A pro-active approach to planning ensures you anticipate customer requirements and establish accurate quantitative data of your capabilities from which to plan to fulfil actual customer requirements as they arise. A response to any specific customer requirement can be put together in a relatively short timescale because the data required is already to hand. You will find little difficulty assessing your ability to meet and respond to any enquiry because you will have up-to-date data at all times. It is only by adopting a pro-active approach to customer relationships that you will be able to ensure you are able to satisfy the requirements of your customers. Adopting a re-active approach to customer enquiries will probably mean that opportunities slip through your hands to better prepared competitors.

The following steps are the key to pro-active planning:

- define your current business activities and current capabilities
- define the areas in which you expect to operate in the foreseeable future and how you will develop the necessary skills and resources to do so
- assess the technical and commercial resources needed to service specific customer needs
- define the operating procedures you need to meet specific customer needs
- quantify additional skills and resources you might need
- develop operating plans to ensure you are ready to fulfil the contract should it be awarded to you
- record the review process, with conclusions and actions taken
- analyse successes and failures to learn how to improve your ability to respond to customer enquiries.

Being pro-active means you will be prepared for the business that is to come. You will have a clear understanding of your capabilities and weaknesses. This gives you a basis for developing your ability to meet perceived future customer requirements.

## A RE-ACTIVE APPROACH

The re-active organisation sees planning as a necessary evil, at best. It will seek ways to minimise the effort; or, as such organisations tend to describe it, minimise the cost of planning.

The re-active organisation waits until a customer order arrives before it begins to rush round in an attempt to respond before the deadline. Re-active planning generally follows the following steps:

- receive details of customer requirements
- internal estimates of costs/times/resources put together
- planning undertaken on how to fulfil the terms of the contract
- assessment of customer expectations of cost/delivery
- discussion of possible difficulties in meeting defined customer requirements
- production of a costed quotation for submission to customer
- a proposal or quotation is produced addressing each of the contract requirements.

Re-active organisations are always under pressure to respond because deadlines are usually short. Their cost estimates are often inaccurate because they have little quantitative data. Their time is spent purely responding to the contract, not anticipating alternatives which might better meet the customer requirements.

Anyone who has been involved in putting together an estimate for a new contract will know the difficulties that are frequently experienced within re-active organisations:

- each function will establish what is required from them
- they will then estimate the cost in time and materials to achieve the contract requirements
- most will refer to previous estimates
- most will agree that these estimates are unreliable and make an allowance 'for contingencies'. These will rarely be supported by real data, and frequently will not be declared
- as the estimate filters up the organisation different managers add their own view to the estimate
- the final management review almost always reduces the bid to increase the possibility of obtaining the business!

Very few of the above decisions will have been based on real data.

Clear planning is the cornerstone to achieving satisfactory business performance.

## SO WHAT DO YOU NEED TO PLAN YOUR BUSINESS?

Any business requires certain key information to enable it to understand and plan to meet customer requirements:

(i)   you will clearly need to understand the skills, facilities and capabilities of your business. Most businesses know broadly what they are capable of, but few assess and document this in a structured way. If you document your capabilities and ensure it is regularly updated, you will ensure you can provide a speedy and accurate response to requests from customers. It also enables management to picture where it is at present and to make plans to control future developments;

(ii)  you will only be able to make an accurate assessment of the likely cost of providing a product or serrvice if you have an effective system for costing the inputs you use; and

66

(iii) you should also ensure you implement a mechanism for statutory health and safety requirements which have an impact on your business. This minimises the time it takes to produce a meaningful response to a contract when this is required.

So how can you record the capability of your business? Many organisations produce a comprehensive statement of their capabilities. This should document the services they are able to provide, the resources and skills they have to support those services and any limits on their abilities. It is also useful to understand the costs involved in providing specific services as this can be used as a basis for assessing the potential profitability of specific contracts.

Once you have produced your capability statement it is a relatively easy task to respond to individual customer requirements. Too many organisations take on a contract and worry about how they will meet the requirements later. An effective QMS enables you understand and plan to fulfil every contract before acceptance. This is also a requirement of ISO9000. The business planning process provides you with the necessary data to enable you to achieve this.

# Agreeing requirements with customers

There are a number of important reasons for producing a formal statement defining the product or service you will provide to your customer:

(i)    it confirms the contractual arrangements you have entered into;

(ii)   it can be used as a basis for checking that your product or service conforms to requirements;

(iii)  it provides a basis for defining the requirements to other departments which were not party to the original negotiations;

(iv)   it will assist you to resolve later disputes, if they arise; and

(v)    it can be used as the baseline against which any changes to the original agreement can be negotiated.

You may choose to define your agreement in a number of ways, such as a letter of engagement, a purchase order or a contract.

Every contract establishes a number of rights and obligations on both parties. It is important to go into any contract with your eyes open. You need to review the terms of the agreement to determine:

- if you are able to provide what is wanted

- if you are prepared to provide the product or service in accordance with the contract as it stands. Would you need more time? Would you need more money to make a profit? Have you got the facilities and the skills?

It is important to review all contracts to ensure you agree to the terms:

- consider contracts which are separately negotiated and those that are the result of standard trading terms, such as between a bank or a major store and the general public

- take account of the after-sales position as well as the initial supply of the product or service. You will clearly need to assess your ability and willingness to support the delivered product or service. Any conditions which you wish to introduce should be defined at the review stage, understood by both parties, and be documented in the contract before it is signed

- review contracts with customers and suppliers.

It is important that for all contracts you have a system to handle any changes which may arise once the initial contract has been agreed. You need to ensure that amendments to a contract are reviewed in the same way as the original contract was reviewed. It is also important that any contract changes agreed can be fed into the system to ensure that only the products or services required by the customer are delivered. Consider the example of a customer who originally negotiated a contract requiring 200 blue boxes to be produced and delivered each fortnight and now wishes to change this to 150 green boxes delivered each week. The contract needs to be reviewed to assess the impact of this, whether you can meet the new requirements, whether you still want the work, the cost of meeting the new requirements, the impact of the changeover and the costs of handling this. Given that you agree to a contract amendment, how will you then handle the change to ensure that from a given date green boxes will be delivered at the rate of 150 per week. What about any work in progress you have, how will you prevent this from being delivered? It is important that your QMS can respond to contract amendments to ensure you fully understand their implications and are capable of meeting the new requirements, before acceptance. This system must ensure that, once accepted, contract amendments can be effectively communicated and transferred to the functions concerned within your organisation to ensure only conforming products and services are delivered.

## SPECIAL CONTRACTS

You should review every customer contract you receive to ensure you are fully capable of meeting the detailed requirements. Reviewing the terms of the agreement will help ensure a satisfactory outcome for the contract. You will have a basis for ensuring that you can fulfil the requirements for all the contracts you accept. If you are not prepared to do the work, whether because you do not have the necessary expertise or the price is too low, you can always decline the contract.

A properly defined review system will ensure that all customer requirements are considered. Failure to operate a contract to the mutual satisfaction of both parties will eventually lead to customer dissatisfaction whatever form the contract takes. You must therefore make sure you are happy with all the terms of the contract before you accept it.

## NORMAL TRADING

69

Many organisations have a system for reviewing 'Special Contracts' but fail to recognise that they also enter into contracts daily with a myriad of smaller customers. Take the example of a garage offering car servicing. It is likely that they will have a number of individually negotiated contracts with companies operating car fleets and, because these contracts are large they are probably thoroughly reviewed before acceptance. The same garage also enters into a contract with every individual who books a car in for service. Both types of contract must be reviewed, the details of the review will be different. For contracts under normal trading terms the review will probably be a simple check against the defined company capabilities before acceptance. The receptionist would probably check that the garage is capable of working on the type of vehicle the customer wants to book in. A garage which services modern cars may well not be capable of servicing a 1920s Chrysler. They should also ensure they can meet the timescales the customer requires. To perform the contract review, the receptionist needs to know it is their responsibility to do this and has to have access to the necessary information.

Many businesses operate normal terms of trade include suppliers of domestic appliances, bus and train services, and power and water supplies. Here the customers usually have little control over the terms of their contract. However, a contract does exist, and the supplier must ensure they understand and meet the requirements of their customers.

Where a formal, written contract is not entered into between a supplier and individual customers, the supplier should identify their perceived 'customer requirements' which they guarantee to meet. This would normally be the responsibility of the marketing operation, supported by whatever resource is appropriate. These requirements should become translated into the standard terms and conditions for the range of products and services offered by the company. Whatever mechanism is used to establish this base-line of defined customer requirements, it is essential that they are applied consistently. They should not be varied at the whim or convenience of the supplier.

Contract Reviews should be conducted by all businesses. They ensure you understand the requirements of your customers and protect you in the event of subsequent disagreement. The procedures for contract review should be clearly defined. Each review should be conducted by qualified individuals and the outcome should be recorded. Any company claiming compliance with ISO9000 must develop and operate procedures to control the contract review process. Remember that the contract review procedures must also be capable of handling contract amendments.

**CHECKLIST: GIVING CUSTOMERS WHAT THEY WANT**

1 Do you operate procedures to review contracts before they are accepted?

2 Who is responsible for co-ordinating the contract review process?

3 Which functions are required to participate in the review process?

4 Who is responsible for resolving problems with your customers?

5 Are the agreed conclusions from the contract review process formally documented?

6 Are records of the review process and its conclusions maintained?

7 Who is responsible for maintaining records within your organisation?

8 How do you ensure that the terms of standard business are included in your review process?

9 How are amendments to contracts reviewed, accepted, communicated and transferred to the functions concerned?

**7**

# Controlling the design process

- ■ **Ensure your designs satisfy customer requirements**
- ■ **Control design changes**
- ■ **Checklist**

## Ensure your designs satisfy customer requirements

The business environment today is intensely competitive. Customers are increasingly demanding. Businesses need to innovate to meet these changing conditions. A new range of Personal Computers may be released annually. Accountants may regularly identify new services, perhaps helping clients solve the lease/buy decision for cars. Banks have relatively recently become involved in the mortgage market, and today a new mortgage service seems to be on offer every month! You may have to regularly introduce new products or services or go out of business.

The quality of your designs will have a significant impact on the future success of your business. A good design in the right market at a competitive price could significantly boost your profitability. A design that fails to meet customer requirements or is difficult to produce could have the opposite effect.

It is therefore important that your design activities are properly focused and managed.

> Note: ISO9001 defines the requirements for design and data control in paragraph 4.4.

The key to a successful product is a good design. Poor production can devastate a good design but the production process can do little to improve a design that is inadequate.

Successful designs require interaction between marketing, design and production teams:

- marketing ensures you understand the anticipated requirements of customers
- production ensures the product or service can be provided
- design translates the requirements into a product or service that can be produced and supported by the organisation.

The first step is to ensure you understand and document your customers' requirements and then control the design process so these are met.

The design process translates specified or implied requirements into instructions that will define the product or service required. You will need to operate procedures to control and verify the design activities so that all specified requirements are met. Control of the design process is critical to the successful production of conforming goods and services. The objective is to ensure you satisfy the requirements of your customers at minimum cost to yourself. The design procedures and codes of practice should be documented and form part of your controlled Quality System.

## DESIGN CONTROL

You will only be able to design products and services which conform to the requirements of your customers and your organisation if you control the design process from initial input to final verification. The objective of design control is to produce:

- a structured design
- that meets the requirements of your customers
- which can be made
- within the cost/time constraints allowed.

Eight key elements affect the quality of the design process. The QMS should define and document the procedures you operate to control each of these elements:

(i)   organisation of the design function. It is essential that everyone understands their role in the design process;

(ii)  planning the design process;

(iii)  defining design inputs to ensure customer requirements are identified;

(iv)  defining design outputs to ensure they fully define the product or service;

(v)  design review procedures for all functions concerned to review the design output at appropriate stages in the design process;

(vi)  verification procedures to ensure the design output meets the input requirements. The designed product or service should meet the requirements of your customers and your employees who have to produce and support the product or service;

(vii)  validation procedures to ensure the product or service designed functions as required under defined operating conditions; and

(viii)  controlling design changes to ensure their impact on the design is assessed before implementation.

Many organisations document their policy and methodology for controlling the design of products and services in a design manual.

## ORGANISATION OF THE DESIGN FUNCTION

One key to a successful design team is to ensure the individuals involved are competent and understand their roles and responsibilities. The following issues should be addressed in the QMS:

- *Structure*: Organisation charts, team descriptions and job descriptions should be used to help individuals understand their role within their team, and to help teams to understand their role within the design function.

- *Competencies*: A design group should have the technical and communication skills to enable it to:
  - understand customer requirements
  - extract further details of customer requirements if necessary
  - understand how the product or service is to function
  - understand how it is to be produced and serviced
  - translate the design inputs into design outputs
  - document the design activities and decisions accurately.

It is not uncommon to find designs that cannot be produced at all, or can only be produced by incurring excessive costs. Specifying materials of non-standard sizes or defining processes with a high manual input are just two examples of failures to design for lowest cost production. The importance of ensuring your designers are competent cannot be overstated.

- *Responsibilities*: The structure defines the roles and responsibilities of individuals and teams within the design function. Responsibilities are, however, meaningless without the associated authority and resources to perform those tasks. The design activity requires adequate resources to enable it to operate effectively. Their requirements include accommodation and equipment, access to up-to-date information, and the opportunity to update skills and experience when required.

- *Interfaces*: Many organisations use a number of small teams each working on a small part of the overall design. When individuals or groups work on part of an overall task, the most important (and difficult) area to control is the interface between the groups. The QMS should document how interfaces between teams are defined and how information is communicated across these interfaces in a controlled way.

76

## PLANNING

Planning is critical to the control of the design process. If an activity is not planned then it cannot be managed. The purpose of design planning is to ensure that all the activities are understood, planned for and monitored throughout the design process. The aim being to reduce the risk of producing non-conforming outputs at any stage in the process.

Design planning should enable you to:

- break complex design projects down into individual modules which can be designed as stand alone elements and then integrated to produce a complete system design

- define discrete design activities and establish responsibilities for their execution

- assign appropriate technical resources to the total design task

- define the design teams and how they should interact

- verify that the design output satisfies the input requirements before the design is released for production

- validate the product or service to ensure it functions as required by users, before release

■ document the design process for each product or project.

If the design process requires multi-disciplinary teams or outside agencies, the interface between these groups should be defined, documented and controlled. A formal Quality Plan can help to ensure you control the design process where external groups are involved. This Plan would define the interfaces between your organisation and the external agency, and the controls you would exercise over their design activity.

No matter where or by whom the design process is conducted, it is a requirement of the Standard, and good management practice to ensure that every activity is planned, documented and recorded. It is important to keep adequate records so that:

(i)   you have a record of the design activities carried out;

(ii)  you can demonstrate that the work was actually carried out as planned;

(iii) you have a record of the total design and basis on which decisions were made about changes to the design;

(iv)  you have data on which to base future decisions. Any lessons learned from this design can be used to guide future designs; and

(v)   you have a basis which would enable you to build on existing designs in the future.

The QMS should define the record-keeping requirements for the design activities. All design records should be retained. They should not be edited. Iteration is a common feature of design activities. Records of past decisions and tests may be used as a basis for enhancing existing designs or developing new ones. Designers' notebooks, minutes of meetings, operational plans, design reviews, verification tests, all form a part of the history of the design and will enable you to trace decisions and assess data long after the design phase is over.

## DESIGN INPUT

A completed design can only conform to the requirements if the requirements are fully understood at the beginning of the design process. It is, therefore, essential to control and document the design inputs, including:

■ customer specifications and requirements

■ statutory requirements for the product and business sector

- the marketplace in which the design output will be released

- the requirements of your production and support departments

- standards for both the design output and the product which will be produced from the design.

Design input is the process of identifying the requirements of your customers (from market research or from contract review) and the requirements of your production and support departments (often from your capability statement).

One of the principal reasons given for not documenting design inputs is that the requirements change as the design progresses, so it is pointless to document the requirements at the beginning. This is a fallacy.

Designing is often an iterative process. Compromises have to be made between conflicting requirements as the design progresses. For example, when designing a PC, requirements may initially be specified for both the speed of the processor and the final cost of the machine. These requirements may prove irreconcilable and a compromise will have to be made once the design team produces factual information on defining what can be achieved against each parameter. Defining target requirements for key parameters is important as a basis for directing the design activity. It also provides a baseline from which future decisions can be made. In the absence of an adequate specification of input requirements, individuals within the design team may define the key parameters for themselves. These may not match the requirements of your customers.

Two factors are vital to success in this area. Dialogue with customers ensures they are aware of both progress and difficulties in achieving the original design objectives. Changes to the design planning documents, or to the design requirements, should be agreed and fully documented.

A wide range of features make up a product and constitute design input. Such features might include:

- performance objectives

- reliability

- maintainability

- size

- weight

- shape

- colour
- interchangeability with other components or equipment
- legal, health and safety requirements.

Where requirements cannot be understood or are ambiguous they must be resolved with your customer. A full understanding of customer requirements can often result from an effective contract review activity; the results of contract review must, therefore, be fed into the design process.

Many products and services are designed by businesses to fulfil a general market requirement. For example, a bank might design and launch a new saving deposit service which it believes it will sell to a large number of individual customers. Here the data on customer requirements is based on market surveys designed to identify anticipated customer requirements. It is important that you apply the same controls to the design process for this type of design project. Here 'customer requirements' would be defined within your company and should be 'owned' by a function with no direct responsibility for the design process or its subsequent production. This would normally be the marketing department. The QMS should define the agreed method, responsibilities and accountabilities for ensuring this activity is adequately performed.

79

## DESIGN OUTPUT

The design output is not the delivered product or service. It is the information from which the delivered product or service is produced. It is important that you define the output you require from the design process. Design output should be sufficient to enable the design to be produced and serviced. You should also ensure the design output meets the design requirements and that objective evidence is available to demonstrate this.

The design output should define or refer to acceptance criteria for the product. These criteria should ensure your design meets the requirements of your customer and your production department. There are two principal types of acceptance critera. Design acceptance criteria define the customer and production requirements which must be met before the design can be released for production. Production acceptance criteria are the criteria which the production department uses to assess whether the product has been produced as designed.

Tests applied as part of the design proving process are frequently more stringent than for production items. This applies particularly to safety and performance tests. This helps ensure that the variability inherent in subsequent production does not lead to a failure to meet the input requirements.

The design output should be fully documented. This may take the form of a report, calculations, specifications or drawings, depending on the product or service. This information should be capable of being understood and used by technical or commercial personnel. It should therefore be clear, easy to understand and unambiguous, and must be reviewed prior to release. The Quality Management System should define the format for the design output.

The design output documentation should identify the project or product to which it relates, and record the identity of the 'designer'. It should also define:

- the characteristics of the new product or service
- production methods
- the design acceptance criteria
- test or verification methods applied in production that are, in effect, proving the design integrity
- appropriate regulatory requirements for the product, regardless of whether these have been explicitly stated in the contract
- the characteristics of the design/product that affect safety and correct functioning. This is becoming increasingly important as a result of increasingly complex product liability legislation.

## DESIGN REVIEWS

As part of the design process, ISO9001 requires design reviews to be carried out at appropriate stages; it is part of your organisation's QMS and design planning to determine at what stages in a given design activity design reviews will be carried out. Design reviews are an important and effective method to verify that the design output meets the input requirements. The purpose of design reviews is to ensure the design develops in such a way that design output will meet the design requirements. Design reviews should be systematic and scheduled. They might be phased to coincide with the achievement of major steps such as feasibility, module design, system integration, manufacture of pre-production models, or final design release for production or delivery to the customer. Design reviews generally take the form of a meeting involving all functions involved in the activity, which subjects the design to a critical evaluation. Typical questions that the review might seek to answer include:

- have we followed the design plan?
- have marketing defined their requirements?
- have the production and support departments defined their requirements?
- have we followed the design procedures?
- do we agree with the findings of the design team?
- does the design stand up to a critical review?
- do we agree with the design team's assumptions?
- do we agree that the design meets the input requirements? Has this been adequately proven?

If the answer to any of these questions is no, then the review team should define the actions required to overcome the deficiency. The detailed questions asked will change as the design progresses. The purpose of the review remains the same: to ensure the design procedures have been followed and you are confident that the design meets the input requirements.

The QMS should ensure that design reviews:

- are planned
- occur throughout the design process
- ensure design objectives are achieved
- ensure changes to output requirements have been authorised
- include representatives from all relavent functions
- are recorded.

Design reviews should be identified in the 'design and development plan' along with the resources for conducting the review. Reviews should be conducted by individuals competent to judge the elements under review who have not had direct involvement with the work being reviewed. It is frequently necessary to use a review team with members drawn from different departments to ensure the design conforms to all the requirements:

- marketing to ensure customer requirements are met
- production and support to ensure the product or service can be produced and supported
- design to carry out a technical assessment and ensure procedures have been followed.

The composition of the design review team may change during the design cycle:

| Design phase | Design team composition |
| --- | --- |
| Concept definition | Design, marketing and production |
| Feasibility study | Design teams |
| Pre-production | Production may chair a team of design and production |
| Final design release | Production and design |

The QMS should clearly define the objectives for each of the formal design reviews, and should specify:

- who is obliged to attend reviews
- the responsibilities of each of the attendees
- the records to be kept for each meeting.

## DESIGN REVIEW RECORDS

Records provide evidence that a review has taken place as planned and provide a summary of the review process, the actions required and the decisions taken. Records of design reviews should show:

- the product/project
- the review participants
- the design aspects addressed by the review
- the conclusions reached and the corrective actions recommended.

A number of issues need to be addressed during each review. You may find it helpful to develop a checklist to ensure these issues are all addressed. These lists should form part of the procedural documentation for the control of the design process.

**A TYPICAL DESIGN REVIEW CHECKLIST**

1  Do design output documents fully reflect the design input requirements?

2  Will the product's performance fully meet reliability and maintainability requirements under expected conditions of use?

3  Is the product safe under all reasonable conditions of use?

4  Does the product comply with legislative requirements?

5  Are the specified materials available and suitable?

6  Are the tolerances and performance requirements achievable?

7  Can the product arising from the design be adequately assembled, tested and serviced?

8  Have acceptance/rejection criteria been adequately specified?

9  Have the necessary user instructions been produced?

10  Does the design permit easy fault diagnosis and repair?

11  Has user feedback from similar product been incorporated in the design?

12  How does the design compare with the competition?

13  Have the requirements for storage, protection, identification and traceability been defined?

14  What allowance has been made in the design verification and testing arrangements for the use of data from similar designs? Has this data been assessed by an independent individual or group?

83

## DESIGN VERIFICATION

Having designed the new product or service it is important to verify that the design output meets the input requirements. Design verification procedures should ensure that adequate evidence is produced to prove that the input requirements at each design stage have been satisfied. ISO9001 provides some guidance regarding the minimum controls to be effected.

It is important that the design verification activity is planned at the start of the design project. The plan should specify when in the design process verification will take place, and also the methods which will be used. When the design is broken down into modules, it is generally more effective to verify that each module conforms with its requirements before integrating them. It is then necessary to verify that the whole system conforms to requirements.

In addition to carrying out design reviews, you may use a number of additional methods to verify designs. Each is appropriate in different circumstances. ISO9001 refers to some of the principal methods:

- undertaking tests and demonstrations
- carrying out alternative calculations
- comparison of new design with similar proven designs.

## QUALIFICATION TESTS

Here, samples of the product or service are taken at various stages in the design process and tested to ensure they conform to the input requirements. These tests should be planned and scheduled in the design plan. The plan should ensure the business is capable of carrying out the tests competently. The plan should define the tests to be carried out and the acceptance criteria.

Qualification tests are designed to ensure that the design output meets the technical requirements. They do not assess conformance to all the input requirements. Accordingly the results of qualification tests should only be used as one source of information to judge design acceptability.

## ALTERNATIVE CALCULATIONS

Alternative calculations may be used to demonstrate the validity of the original calculation. If you are writing software you may use manual calculations to ensure your program produces the expected results. The applicability of alternative calculations should be decided at the beginning of the design project and included in the design plan.

## COMPARISON WITH PROVEN DESIGNS

Comparison with similar proven designs would be another way to provide some evidence of the adequacy of the design calculations and methodology.

The QMS should define the procedures which you use to verify that design output meets the input requirements. It should specify at what stages verification is carried out, what methods are used and what records are maintained.

## DESIGN VALIDATION

Design validation follows successful design verification and is intended to demonstrate that the product or service conforms to defined user requirements under defined operating conditions. Design validation is a separate and different activity to design verification. Design verification involves the verification that design output meets design input requirements; it can be performed on design output documentation which defines the 'theoretical design',

Design validation is generally performed on the final product or service and is related to the intended use of the product or service. Validation ensures that the product or service is demonstrably suitable for its intended use. Typical validation methods may include:

85

- prototype testing
- commissioning trials
- trial marketing of a product or service.

Although validation is usually carried out on the final product or service this may not always be possible. Also multiple validations may be required if there are different intended uses.

Together, verification and validation confirm the compliance of the design with the input requirements and with the final user application.

# Design changes

Designs are not static. They evolve throughout the design process. They may also be developed post release, as businesses continually seek to satisfy the changing requirements of their customers.

No matter how trivial a change request may appear it will, if implemented, change the original design. The change may improve some aspects of performance, but others may be adversely affected. The QMS should ensure that any proposed changes are fully assessed to consider their impact on the proven design. The QMS should ensure that:

- change requests from whatever source are identified
- the impact of any change is evaluated
- additional design proving is undertaken where appropriate
- appropriate approval is obtained before a change is implemented
- changes are fully documented.

Any proposed change to the design must be subject to adequate technical review to assess its impact on the overall product or service before the design change is approved and implemented.

Your responsibility is to ensure you have new designs that work, can be produced and fully meet customer requirements. This may involve the development of new designs and adapting proven designs to meet new circumstances. ISO9001 defines sensible procedures for ensuring that your designs meet customer requirements, and can be produced and supported by your organisation.

**CHECKLIST: CONTROLLING THE DESIGN PROCESS**

**Organisation**

1 Have you defined your design organisation?

2 Have you defined the responsibilities and authorities for teams and individuals?

3 How do you ensure the competence of the design organisation?

**Design and development planning**

1 Do you prepare a plan for each design project?

2 In what form are your design/development plans drawn up?

3 Do you have a methodology for breaking down a design into modules? How is this documented?

4 Do your plans identify responsibilities and authorities for each activity?

5 Are your plans controlled and updated as necessary?

6 Has responsibility for design verification been assigned?

7 Do your design plans define organisational and technical interfaces between design groups?

8 How do you control the transfer of data transfer across interfaces?

**Design input**

1 How do you document design input requirements?

2 Have you identified the individuals responsible for reviewing design input requirements for adequacy?

3 How does your system identify regulatory requirements?

## Design output

1 What form do design outputs take and how are they controlled?

2 Do design outputs contain acceptance criteria?

3 How do you ensure regulatory requirements are met?

4 Do your design outputs identify safety critical characteristics?

5 How do you identify the product/service and the designer in design outputs?

## Design verification

1 Are verification activities identified and included in the design plan?

2 How do you ensure verification personnel are qualified and competent?

3 How do you define the verification methods and acceptance criteria?

4 Do you carry out design reviews? Are the methods and criteria documented?

## Design validation

1 Are validation activities identified and included in the design plan?

2 Is there a validation plan defining how the activity will be performed and the acceptance criteria?

3 Has the plan been accepted by, or on behalf of, the customer?

4 Are the validation results corroborated and reviewed?

## Design changes

1 How are design change requests documented?

2 Have you identified personnel responsible for reviewing changes before acceptance?

3 Are the methods used for reviewing changes documented? Do they include reference to the original design data and the re-running of appropriate verification tests, if required?

4 Do you ensure you obtain customer approval, when required?

5 Is your design change system sufficiently flexible to cater for changes both pre- and post-release from the design phase?

6 How can you identify the current design status?

# 8

# Managing your suppliers

- Specify what you want
- Control your purchasing activity
- Select your suppliers
- Monitor supplier performance
- Action plan
- Checklist

## Specify what you want

You are responsible for ensuring that the products and services you supply conform to the requirements of your customers at minimum cost.

No doubt you buy in goods or services from external suppliers. These may be used directly as part of the product or service delivered to your customers, or they may be used to support your internal processes. For example, in a kitchen, the chef will require fresh meat and vegetables as a basis for his cooking. He will also require an oven. Although the oven is not actually delivered to his customer the chef needs it to cook on. Your ability to meet the needs of your external customers will frequently depend on the goods and services you receive from your external suppliers. Controlling the procurement activity is an essential part of your Quality Management System.

Most businesses suffer because they accept the supply of goods or services that do not conform to their requirements. It is often easier to attempt to compensate for poor suppliers rather than take steps to

Note: ISO9001 defines the requirements for procurement in paragraphs 4.6 and 4.10.

improve their performance. However, the use of poor suppliers can have a significant impact on your ability to meet your customers' requirements at minimum overall cost. Holding excess inventory, living with excessive lead-times, making do with equipment that is less than satisfactory or engaging in extensive on-receipt inspection activities. All these have a significant impact on the costs you bear and hence the efficiency of your business.

You must ensure that you manage your suppliers so you only receive goods and services that conform to *your* requirements.

This is the purpose of an effective Quality Management System. An effective QMS ensures that you only receive goods and services from suppliers which meet your requirements. The following key elements need to be controlled:

(i)   control your purchasing activity;

(ii)  select your suppliers carefully; and

(iii) monitor supplier performance to ensure you only receive conforming goods or services.

90

# Control your purchasing activity

You will only receive conforming products and services from your suppliers if you are able to define your requirements fully, clearly and unambiguously. More than 50 per cent of purchasing errors are frequently due to an inadequate specification of requirements by the purchaser. They are not due to incompetence on the part of the supplier. They are due to incompetence on the part of the purchasing organisation.

When you purchase goods or services it is only you that knows exactly what you want. If you do not adequately define your requirements, you are unlikely to get exactly what you want. It takes time and energy to resolve problems with suppliers. It is your responsibility to ensure that problems do not arise.

It is, therefore, essential that your QMS ensures all orders are placed in a consistent manner and specify the data required to fully define the product or service you want. The following specific types of data are generally required in any purchase order:

- technical specification
- quality requirements
- delivery, cost and commercial terms.

## TECHNICAL SPECIFICATION

A detailed description of the product or service should cover the essential performance parameters. Wherever possible, the purchase order should refer to specific part numbers, drawings, specifications, proposals or reports to describe the items required in such a manner that the requirements cannot be misinterpreted.

It is important to avoid using descriptions such as 'blue', 'scratch-free', 'rapid' or 'efficient'. These terms are meaningless. It is not possible to determine whether or not a product or service actually meets these requirements.

If you purchase meat for a kitchen, asking for 'lean' or 'fresh' beef allows your supplier to interpret what you mean. They may have a very different interpretation to your own! Specifying 'less than 5 per cent total fat' and 'hanging for no more than $x$ days' leaves no room for misinterpretation. Conformance to these requirements can be measured if required.

If you have trouble trying to define a parameter, try asking the question 'how would conformance to this parameter be measured?'. This will generally ensure that the parameter is adequately described.

The purchase order should also define any special requirements which you want the supplier to meet when fulfilling the order, such as:

- special processes
- codes of practice
- personnel.

For example, if you are procuring a training course, you may specify the parameters of the course in terms of:

- content of the course
- duration
- numbers of attenders
- experience of attenders
- dates of courses.

You may also wish to specify the qualifications, or even sometimes the names, of the individuals who will deliver the course.

It is your job to ensure that you get what you want.

## QUALITY REQUIREMENTS

If you want your supplier to conform to specific quality requirements then these must be detailed on the purchase order. Examples might include:

- the supplier must conform to a specific quality standard (such as ISO9001)

- specific inspection or test procedures must be carried out

- specific records are to be kept to demonstrate compliance with defined procedures

- for large contracts you may want the supplier to provide details of specific processes, controls, inspection and test procedures, their principal suppliers and records for your contract. These are frequently detailed in a specific Quality Plan for the contract or order. The requirement for a Quality Plan must be included in the purchase order

- some of your external customers may specify requirements which apply to your suppliers. For example, a customer may specify that all suppliers should hold a recognised quality system approval, or they may reserve the right to carry out inspection activities at your supplier. Your QMS should recognise specific customer requirements and ensure they are included on purchase orders

- acceptance criteria defining the way in which conformance to requirements will be measured. This ensures that both the purchaser and supplier determine acceptance against the same criteria. This avoids problems which could arise if different methods were used by the supplier and customer.

For example, a technical description for an instrument front panel might state that no defect should be visible when the panel is illuminated. If the description did not specify how to measure acceptable performance, problems could arise. In one instance, the supplier designed a test jig which illuminated the panel from behind, as though it was in use. The supplier looked for defects that would be apparent to users of the instrument. The purchaser used different criteria to determine acceptance and found an unacceptable level of rejects. The purchaser subjected the panel to bright illumination from the front and looked, under a microscope, for defects exceeding a given size. The supplier was unable to reproduce the faults found by the purchaser. In this case a great deal of energy was expended trying to resolve problems which arose because of differences in measuring conformance. Defining acceptance criteria saves time. In the above case, the tests devised by the purchaser were so sensitive that users could not detect the faults it picked up.

The definition of acceptance doesn't mean the purchaser will carry out acceptance tests or inspection. It is the supplier's responsibility to ensure conformance to your requirements and acceptance criteria. However, failure to specify acceptance criteria can lead to a great deal of wasted time and effort.

The costs associated with an inadequate description of your technical and quality requirements may be hidden but are important since they are likely to be high, and they may have an important impact on your ability to meet customer requirements.

93

## DELIVERY, COST AND COMMERCIAL TERMS

It is necessary to include details of quantities, delivery times, pricing required and a definition of the terms of trade between the two organisations. Many businesses already document and control this aspect of order placement well because they understand the cost implications of not defining these clearly.

Your Quality Management System should ensure that an adequate description of your total requirement is specified when an order is placed.

# Select your suppliers

Having determined exactly what you want to purchase you need to select a supplier. Your ability to meet your external customers' requirements may well depend on the ability of your suppliers to meet your requirements. An effective QMS requires a robust and effective system to control the selection of suppliers.

The system should recognise that the level of control required over the procurement activity depends on the influence the procured product or service has on your ability to meet your customer requirements. For example, a training establishment might decide to subcontract both the running and the catering of one of its courses. Running the course is a critical element in its ability to meet its customer requirements and consequently its procurement must be rigorously controlled. The same organisation may decide that the supply of food to delegates is not a critical part of their service. In this case, the procurement activity still needs to be controlled but the supplier selection criteria, and the level of verification may be less stringent.

The method you use to select suppliers should be carefully considered and documented as part of your QMS. The selection process may involve a number of functions within the business:

- finance     – to gauge the financial soundness of your supplier
- purchasing– to negotiate the terms of the agreement
- design     – to ensure the supplier has the capability to meet the technical requirements
- production – to assess the supplier's ability to produce the product or service in accordance with their requirements
- quality     – to assess the supplier's Quality System to ensure conforming products and services are consistently produced.

There are a number of different criteria which can be used as the basis for selecting suppliers:

- past performance
- assessment of their quality system
- assessment of their products and services.

Different criteria may be used in different circumstances. Whatever combination is used, it must be capable of assessing the supplier's ability to meet all your requirements; technical, quality, delivery, cost and commercial.

## PAST PERFORMANCE

Many businesses already have a relationship with a number of suppliers and may have accumulated historical data on their performance. It is important that you collect this data and record it so it can be easily accessed. This information can be very valuable as it can help you assess the likely performance of individual suppliers in the future. Three factors are important when considering past performance as part of this decision making process:

(i)    the data on which the decision is made should be factual and recorded data. You should not base decisions merely on opinion;

(ii)   the product or service required should be similar to that previously supplied; and

(iii)  the supplier should not have been subject to significant changes in the period since the data were measured.

Past performance may include your own experience, or that of other users. It may be useful to call on the experience of others, such as trade organisations or sister companies within your group for information if you have access to them.

## ASSESSMENT OF QUALITY SYSTEM

An assessment of a supplier's quality system can be useful in determining their *potential* ability or willingness to understand and meet your requirements. Many organisations use the DTI register of quality assessed companies to determine whether the supplier holds a recognised National Approval, such as ISO9001, for their quality system. It is important to check that the registration is current and that the scope of the approval covers the products or service which you wish to purchase.

Alternatively you may visit the supplier's premises to review their technical, commercial, and quality procedures in practice. If you assess a potential supplier's quality system as part of the decision making process it is important that the basis for the decision, and the standard against which the system was assessed are recorded. Assessment of the supplier's QMS does, however, only provide a general view of their potential ability to consistently supply the broad type of service or product you want to purchase. It does not assess his actual ability to meet your specific technical requirements.

## PRODUCT OR SERVICE ASSESSMENT

Many businesses ask potential suppliers to produce samples that conform to their requirements. These samples can be assessed to determine conformance to requirements. This method is useful since it determines the supplier's ability to meet your actual requirements. It may also reveal weaknesses in the requirement itself! It should not, however, be used as the sole means of assessment, since it only assesses the ability of the supplier to meet some of the requirements (usually only the technical requirements) at the specific time when the samples were made. This method does not test the supplier's ability to meet *all* the requirements consistently over a period of time.

Each of these selection criteria may be appropriate in different circumstances. Rarely is one criterion sufficient as the basis for a decision. The QMS should define:

- the criteria to use in different circumstances
- who decides which criteria to use
- who is involved in specific supplier assessments
- the records to be kept describing the basis for decisions, who was involved, and the data
- on which the decision was made.

## APPROVED SUPPLIERS

It is important to ensure that individuals who place purchase orders know which suppliers have been approved to supply specific products or services. This information must be recorded in an Approved Suppliers List which typically includes the following information:

- name and address of supplier
- basis on which approval has been given: details of National approvals, on-site assessment and historical data
- date on which approval given and the duration of approval
- scope of services/products for which approval given
- any restrictions.

The QMS should specify the information to include in this list and who is responsible for maintaining and issuing it. Supplier approvals should be subject to regular reviews based on performance and changes in business circumstances. The QMS should describe how the Approved Suppliers List is reviewed, by whom, how often and on what basis.

# Monitor supplier performance

The proof that the goods or services have been supplied in accordance with your requirements comes when this has been verified. There are three key points at which verification can take place:

- at source inspection
- on-receipt inspection
- in-use verification.

With a developing awareness of Quality costs, a focus on meeting customer requirements, at minimum cost, and the focus of the 1994 ISO9000 Standard on preventive actions, the location of an acceptance process either at your supplier's premises or even at receipt within your own organisation is often indicative of a poor supplier selection process. The aim should be to work with suppliers and improve your supplier selection and monitoring process to eliminate this type of verification activity.

## AT SOURCE

Here the purchaser sends his personnel to the supplier's site to test or inspect the products or services before release for despatch. This approach is very costly as the purchaser has to attend the supplier's premises. It may also, if continued for any length of time, reduce the supplier's ownership of the product, perhaps because they feel they lose responsibility for ensuring the product or service conforms to your requirements. There is a real danger that your involvement will be seen as an extension of their quality system, a sort of super final inspection.

This type of inspection can, however, have a limited role at the beginning of a large project or when a supplier has been selected, perhaps because of lack of choice, which does not totally meet the selection criteria.

For inspection at source to be effective it should be seen as a short-term expedient. The objective is to ensure the supplier is able to consistently produce products or services that meet your requirements. It may also be used as a means of improving supplier performance. By detecting deficiencies early you can help to ensure corrective actions are implemented rapidly. This minimises the impact of defects on your business.

This type of inspection shortens the lines of communication between the supplier and customer. This can help ensure problems are resolved as soon as possible.

## ON-RECEIPT INSPECTION

Here products and services are verified on receipt, before being accepted for use by the purchasing organisation. This is another expensive activity which is only required because your supplier does not meet the requirements for which he has been paid!

Not only is on-receipt inspection expensive and often unnecessary but it can also introduce errors into the system. Packing and unpacking Integrated Circuits can subject them to electrostatic damage; painted panels can be scratched; components may be put back into the wrong box.

However, on-receipt inspection can be a useful means of gathering data to enable you to improve the performance of your suppliers. It should only be used until supplier performance has improved to a point where the on-receipt verification is no longer required. This may be the result of improvements by your supplier, or it may result from improvements in the specification of purchasing requirements!

Too often, however, on-receipt verification degenerates to the point where it is used across the board to sort good from bad.

On receipt inspection is only ever required because of failures elsewhere in the system. As such, it should always be a target for reduction.

## IN-USE VERIFICATION

If you adequately define the requirements for goods and services and only select suppliers who will consistently meet those requirements, then there will be no need for pre-use verification. Here, verification will only need to take place at the point of use and the system will be operating at minimum overall cost.

This method has the advantage that responsibility for meeting requirements rests where it most certainly belongs, with your suppliers. You are, after all, paying them to do the job properly.

However, this method does mean that if the system breaks down then errors will not be found until the product or service is in use. This may have serious implications in terms of failing to meet your customers' requirements. This method can, therefore, only be used if you have confidence in the effectiveness of your prevention system. This confidence should be based on factual data.

If failures do occur, they must be investigated rapidly and thoroughly to ensure the root cause is determined and corrective actions implemented to prevent recurrence. If your Quality system is effective then breakdowns should be very rare. Failures should be met with a rapid and positive reaction from your suppliers so errors can be rectified as quickly as possible.

# Action plan

Controlling the procurement activity is complex. There are six key steps in establishing an effective procurement system:

1 Ensure purchasing requirements are fully documented before an order can be placed. Ensure purchase orders define your technical, quality, delivery, commercial and cost requirements.

2 Ensure you carefully select the suppliers you use. Where you have to use suppliers which do not meet your selection criteria, ensure you undertake the necessary verification procedures to compensate and minimise the risks of receiving non-conforming product.

3 Determine the type and level of verification to be used for each supplier/supplied item. Ensure this system minimises total cost by maintaining a balance between the cost of verification and the cost of not detecting errors sufficiently early. Ensure the system is flexible so that changes can be made to the level and type of verification as circumstances change.

4 Maintain records of supplier performance. Use this data to drive supplier improvements and make sensible decisions on the type/level of verification required. The data should also be used to detect areas of weakness and implement improvements to your QMS.

5 Continuously work with suppliers to improve their performance and ensure your procurement system keeps up with their changing circumstances.

6 Document your procurement system taking all the above into account. Your documentation should:

- describe the process
- determine the decisions to be taken throughout the process
- determine who takes those decisions
- determine the data on which decisions are based
- describe the records which need to be kept to support the decisions taken and demonstrate that the QMS has been followed.

99

Documentation is critical. If you do not define your procedures in writing they will not be followed and your Quality Management System will become ineffective.

**CHECKLIST: MANAGING YOUR SUPPLIERS**

**Purchasing data**

**1** Do you operate a documented system for purchasing goods and services? Does this system ensure that all requirements are fully specified?

**2** Does your system ensure that acceptance criteria are specified?

**3** How does your system ensure that any relevent customer requirements are communicated to the supplier?

**4** Does your system ensure that, when required, appropriate quality system standards are fully referenced on the order?

**5** How are changes to orders communicated to your suppliers?

**Selection of suppliers**

**1** How do you select your suppliers?

**2** Do your selection criteria cover technical, quality, delivery, financial and commercial criteria?

**3** Have you established an Approved Supplier List?

**4** How is this list reviewed, updated and communicated to the individuals who place purchase orders?

**5** How do you prevent orders being placed on non-approved suppliers?

**6** What data do you keep to support the selection of suppliers?

**Verification**

**1** What system do you use to determine the level and type of verification to be carried out?

**2** Do you gather information on supplier performance?

**3** Do you analyse this data and use it to amend the level/type of verification carried out?

# 9

# Controlling the production process

## Controlling the production process

Having designed your product or service to meet the requirements of your customers, you must ensure you produce it as intended. You must, therefore, define, document and control the production processes which turn the initial specification into a product or service. An effective Quality Management System incorporates a number of key elements, each of which is included within the ISO9000 requirements:

(i)   plan and define the production processes which translate the specification into a delivered product or service;

(ii)  plan for the maintenance of any equipment essential to the production process. This should include any equipment used in support functions, such as MIS systems;

(iii) ensure that the product or service is identified throughout the production process to prevent the risk of error;

> Note: ISO9001 defines the requirements for controlling identifying and monitoring the production process paragraphs 4.7, 4.8, 4.9, 4.10, 4.11, 4.12, 4.15 and 4.20.

(iv) plan how you will verify that the product meets the requirements of your customers. You may use any suitable means including test, inspection and process monitoring throughout the production process. Whatever methods are selected must be defined, controlled and capable;

(v) plan how you will protect the product or service from damage, deterioration or loss; and

(vi) if the customer supplies any items to be incorporated in the delivered product or service then plan how you will prevent loss, damage or incorrect use.

ISO9000 does not define what has to be done. It only defines the parameters which must be controlled. You are free to implement the most effective system for your organisation.

## PLANNING AND CONTROLLING THE PRODUCTION PROCESS

104 Production is the series of processes which convert the initial specification into a delivered product or service which meets the customer requirements. If it is to be succesful then it must be planned and controlled. When defining the production process two key elements need to be addressed:

- define the series of sequential processes through which a product or service must pass to convert an input into a delivered product or service which conforms to the customer's requirements

- devise a system for recording that any given product or service has passed through the pre- determined series of processes.

You need to develop the most appropriate method for achieving these two requirements within your business.

Manufacturing operations frequently use route cards to define the sequence of production stages. Each card specifies the processes which must be completed, referring to relevent work instructions defining the activities at each stage in the production process. Marking off the route card as each stage is completed establishes a system to identify what stage the job has reached. At the end of the production activity this card provides a record of the total production process.

Similar methods may well be appropriate for other businesses. Many businesses use checklists to plan their work and record what stage it has reached in the process:

- auditors – to monitor the status of each audit
- solicitors – for conveyancing
- tax advisers – to record the status of a tax return
- surveyors – to monitor the status of individual client instructions.

Checklists are a convenient means of controlling professional work. Individuals sign the checklist once they have completed a specified step. The list then provides evidence that procedures have been followed. This enables the product or service to be released at the end of the production process.

Planning and recording progress through production ensures products and services follow the pre-determined route designed to ensure they conform to customer requirements. It also enables anyone else who becomes involved in the assignment to quickly assess what has been done and what remains to complete the production task.

## PRODUCTION SUPPORT

105

When planning the production process, it is also essential to plan how you will support the production process. One of the key elements that is often overlooked is ensuring that all equipment used either directly by the production process, or indirectly to support that process is adequately maintained to prevent breakdown. One essential to consider is the maintenance of computer equipment. If, for instance, a computer system is used to log on orders and the system is often down then either orders cannot be taken, which is frustrating for the customer, or orders are taken manually, often leading to error. It is therefore essential that a maintenance programme is planned and in place for such equipment, fix on fail is not acceptable!

## IDENTIFICATION

It is important that you can identify specific products and services. This enables you to:

(i) ensure you supply the correct product or service to each customer. Within a professional firm it would be highly embarassing to send out a tax computation for a client to another company within the same operating group!

(ii) ensure you can uniquely identify any product or service to ensure you are working on the right one. A motor car manufacturer must know that the special features are being added to the right car. A solicitor must know he is working on the correct file when drawing up a will for Mr Jones!

(iii) ensure you know what stage in the production process the product or service has reached. When conveyancing, there may be little point carrying out a local search if the building survey has not been completed.

The purpose of identification is to minimise the potential for error and hence reduce the risk of non-conformance. Your QMS should define the methods you use to identify products and services. The means you use should ensure that you can uniquely identify any product or service, and identify the current status of each product or service.

The complexity of the method used will depend on your business.

Having defined how you will identify your products or services, you must decide how you will physically relate the identification to the item. Again a number of methods may be appropriate, these include tags, labels, stamping and branding. Any method can be used that is appropriate to your business.

In the food industry, for example, you might decide that an important part of the product identification is the last date for which a product is suitable for use. In this case you might decide to stamp all food items with a 'use-by' stamp. Farmers may tag or brand animals with a unique serial number which can be related back to their description and history.

In an office environment, every letter might have its own unique identification or file reference. When coupled with the date of production this may be adequate to ensure that correspondence is not confused.

## TRACEABILITY

Many businesses need to be able to trace information about how products or services were produced long after they have been delivered to a customer:

■ aircraft manufacturers may need to be able to identify the source of batches of components. If, for example, an aircraft part fails then all similar aircraft would have to be grounded awaiting investigation unless there was an adequate system for tracing components. If you could trace the source and batch number of the failed part you could determine which other aircraft to ground as they included components from the suspect batch. This information could be used to limit the number of aircraft grounded and hence reduce the associated costs

- in the printing industry, colour matches are often important. Records which show the colours used for specific jobs might be essential to the needs of both customer and supplier

- in the food industry it is essential that the source and identity of ingredients used is controlled and recorded

- many businesses would benefit from a system which enabled them to relate products or services to particular production processes. This enables you to investigate the causes of failure and implement corrective actions if defects arise.

In some cases it is not always product traceability that is required. Sometimes it is important to be able to trace processes or people. In the Health Service it can be important to maintain traceability of the people involved in a particular process. Take the case of a doctor identified as carrying hepatitis. Hospital records must be sufficiently detailed to enable all patients he treated to be identified, contacted and screened. Without a means of tracing the individuals potentially at risk, the screening process would be much more complex and costly.

107

The purpose of traceability is to provide a history of the product or service which can be used to make it easier to solve problems that arise later. This reduces the cost of finding a solution if things subsequently go wrong. You may need to keep detailed records to establish an effective system for traceability. ISO9000 requires that traceability is considered and implemented where it is necessary. It is your decision to determine whether traceability is a requirement for your business. Sometimes it will be required by an individual customer; it may be an industry standard; or it may be required by statute.

# Verifying your products and services meet customer requirements

You are responsible for ensuring that the products and services you supply to your customers conform to their requirements. Your QMS should define how you ensure you achieve this objective. ISO9000 does not define the tests and inspection procedures required. However, it does require you to implement a system to provide confidence that processes work as defined: that is right first time, every time. There are two basic approaches to ensuring that products or services conform to requirements:

- you can inspect, measure and test output. This is costly, delays the production process, can introduce errors and does not improve the production processes

- you can ensure you understand the processes which are employed in your business and then control the process parameters so that they produce conforming output. This ensures the processes work as designed and eliminates the cost of inspection and test.

The most effective way to minimise operating costs is to control processes so they are reliable and error free. This minimises the need to inspect and test their output. There is, however, a risk that if the process control breaks down, non-conforming product will carry on through the production process.

At some point, therefore, you may decide to do some testing or inspection. There are three principal stages for inspection and test procedures:

(i)   receiving inspection is carried out before products or services are accepted for use. This is discussed further in Chapter 8;

(ii)  in-process inspection is carried out between production processes. Its purpose is to ensure processes are under control and to prevent the movement of non-conforming product between processes; and

(iii) final inspection is carried out before the product or service is released for delivery. As a minimum, this should ensure that any inspection or tests required earlier in the production process have been carried out.

Your QMS should document your system for controlling output from the production process. It should define how you:

- plan and schedule the tests and inspections required
- define the purpose of each test and the method and equipment to be used
- identify who is responsible for carrying out the tests
- decide the criteria for passing or failing the test
- decide the actions to be taken once the inspection has been carried out

- specify the records that are to be kept
- identify passed and failed items.

Tests and inspections should be planned and scheduled. They should be conducted by staff of adequate competence and integrity. This involves more than just technical training. It also requires clear leadership from management. Management should demonstrate their commitment to the test and inspection procedures. Employees should know that test results will not be compromised by the need to achieve a particular result on a given day. If management are guilty of this then they might as well give up now since their QMS will have no credibility within the organisation.

Every test and inspection should be conducted in accordance with the planned schedule, and the results recorded. These records have two purposes.

(i) they provide evidence that the test or inspection has been carried out. They also enable the recorded results to be checked if, for any reason, there is reason to doubt the information or the validity of the test; and

(ii) the data can be used to measure trends in performance. This analysis can be useful for corrective action purposes. For this reason the practice of recording a simple 'pass' or 'fail' should be avoided. Ensure that empirical results of measurements are recorded, where possible. This information can enable you to detect if a process is moving towards its control limits and is about to produce non-conforming output. This sort of empirical data is an important basis for investigating the root cause of the problems.

## INSPECTION AND TEST STATUS

It is important to ensure that non-conforming products or services are not allowed to mix with conforming products. If they are allowed to mix then the whole purpose of performing the test will be lost.

It is therefore necessary to distinguish items which have passed the inspection from those that have failed. This is the test status of the product. There are a number of ways of indicating the test/inspection status. The most usual means are:

- applying a stamp or label
- signing a checklist or route card

109

■ use of inspection locations.

Many businesses use a combination of these methods. The key requirement is that any individual involved in the process should be able to determine unambiguously whether the product has passed, failed, or has not yet been subject to the required test or inspection. It should not be possible to move an item to another process if either the required test/inspection has not been carried out, or if the result was unsatisfactory.

Inspection and test requirements are frequently included in the records used for defining the production path. Manufacturing route cards may include details of any inspection or test procedures required. Including a space on the card to record the results of the test fulfils the requirement to record the inspection status of the product. Similarly, a checklist may describe the sequence of activities to be carried out during a house conveyance; a space on the checklist for signature once the activity has been carried out will indicate its status at any time during the process.

## INSPECTION MEASURING AND TEST EQUIPMENT

Many organisations rely on equipment to measure or test process output. You must ensure measuring and test equipment is capable of performing the job demanded of it. The purpose of calibration is to provide confidence in any decisions that are based on measurement data. There are two requirements you must fulfil: you must use the right equipment, and you must ensure the equipment is properly calibrated so you can rely on its results. Equipment should be regularly checked against appropriate standards and adjusted if necessary. These calibrations should be certified by competent organisations which are able to trace the validity of their standards to the absolute measurement defined by national and international standards. In the UK, National Standards are held at the National Physical Laboratory.

If measurement systems are inaccurate then measurements will be inaccurate. The conclusions and decisions resulting from these measurements may well be wrong. If you use inaccurate equipment, you will not be able to ensure customer requirements are met.

To control the measurement activity so you are confident in the results requires three key steps:

(i)   define what measurements are required. Measurements may be required throughout the business: in procurement, in the production process, or during the design verification process;

(ii) define the methods and equipment to be used for each measurement; and

(iii) define the accuracy required for each measuring instrument. From this you can define procedures for ensuring equipment is regularly calibrated so it is capable of performing the tasks required at all times. *All* equipment and systems used for the assessment and checking of deliverable product or services must be subjected to a documented and audited calibration system.

Once you have identified your equipment measurement requirements, you will need to document your calibration system to address the following:

■ how you identify equipment, its accuracy, its calibration status and the date it requires re-calibration

■ how you ensure that, once calibrated, adjustments cannot be made locally which will affect its accuracy

■ how you recall equipment which is due for calibration

■ how you adjust the periodicity of equipment re-calibration

■ the records which you will maintain.

If on presenting equipment for calibration it has already moved outside the accuracy you require then you will need to adjust the interval between calibrations, and determine what actions you need to take to check the reliability of measurements taken on this equipment since the last calibration. This may involve withdrawing suspect items and repeating the measurements.

Surveys of public opinion and other methods of measuring parameters all need to be subject to controls to ensure their accuracy. This usually requires control of the methods used, the people authorised to carry out the measurements and the techniques used to analyse the results.

It is important to calibrate the accuracy of public opinion or market surveys where possible. The results of political polls can be compared with the results of elections. An explanation should be found for any differences. This information should be used to revise the poll procedures, if appropriate, so a more reliable result can be obtained in future. This may be achieved by adjusting the sample size, the nature of the sample or the questions asked.

111

## STATISTICAL TECHNIQUES

Statistical techniques are widely used as a means of analysing data. Statistical sampling, at its simplest, is the examination of the characteristics of a sample from a population. The results from this sample are used as a basis for describing the expected characteristics of the whole population.

Stastical Process Control (SPC) is founded on the concept that the most efficient way to control the output from a process is to control the process that produces the output. Analysing the process by assessing changes and trends in small samples of the output as the process is operating enables corrections to be made to the process controls before non-conforming output is produced.

ISO9000 states that if statistical methods are used then they should be understood, controlled and soundly based. When documenting your system for controlling statistical techniques you should cover the following:

- identification of appropriate techniques
- document when and how these techniques should be used
- ensure that the techniques are used by competent trained personnel
- ensure that, whenever possible, the techniques used are based on recognised, published methods, such as BS6001 for statistical sampling.

# Protecting your products

You are responsible for ensuring that the products and services delivered to your customers meet their requirements. You will therefore have to devise effective means of protecting your products from damage, deterioration or loss. This may include:

- protection from physical damage
- protection from electrical discharge which can totally destroy sensitive electronic circuits
- protection of food during handling and storage. Is it stored in clean containers and covered against contamination? Are the store keepers clean and healthy? Are their washrooms up to standard? Are they trained to handle food correctly? Is food at correct temperatures to ensure preservation?

■ security is often at the top of the list when assessing protection measures during storage. However most businesses control this aspect reasonably well

■ you also need to minimise deterioration and contamination during storage by adequate stock checking and stock control procedures

■ packaging should adequately protect the product within the company and during its delivery to the customer. This may also require the control of packing suppliers

■ you also need to ensure you make adequate arrangements to ensure safe, accurate delivery of products and services.

The methods you adopt to control the handling, packaging, storage and delivery of your products and services should be documented in your Quality Management System.

# Customer supplied products

113

Your customers may supply you with products (perhaps special components), equipment (perhaps a special test jig) or information (perhaps data for a client's tax return) for you to use in your business. You must develop a system to prevent loss, damage or incorrect use of any items supplied to you by your customer for incorporation into their product. The system adopted should:

■ ensure you verify and identify the items supplied

■ protect against damage, deterioration or loss

■ ensure the item is only used as authorised by the customer

■ ensure the customer is informed if any item is lost or damaged whilst in your care.

---

## CHECKLIST: CONTROLLING THE PRODUCTION PROCESS

**Production process control**

1 How do you define and document the processes for producing products or services?

2 How is passage through the process recorded?

3 Have you built into the process requirement the need for identification?

4 Have you built into the process the need for verification?

5  Have you planned maintenance for production and support equipment? Does this include your MIS systems?

**Identification and traceability**

1 What method have you established to unambiguously identify products and services?

2 How is the product or service physically marked to identify it?

3 Is traceability a requirement for your business? If it is a requirement, what procedures do you operate?

**Inspection and test**

1 Have you planned your inspection and test requirements? On what basis were your decisions made? Have you considered on-receipt, in process and final inspection?

2 Have you documented the methods equipment and personnel to carry out inspection and test activities?

3 Have you established acceptance criteria and what actions need to be taken once the inspection/test has been completed?

4 How do you identify items that are untested, passed and failed?

5 What inspection and test records do you keep?

6 How do you ensure that uninspected or failed product cannot move to the next process?

## Calibration

1 Have you determined the measurement requirements of your business and the methods, equipment and accuracies that these require?

2 How do you identify your measuring equipment and how/where it can be used?

3 How do you ensure that your equipment is regularly calibrated against known standards traceable to National Standards?

4 How do you identify the period for which each item of equipment is within calibration?

5 How do you recall equipment which is due for re-calibration?

6 How do you determine and adjust the calibration periodicity?

7 How do you prevent unauthorised adjustments to equipment?

8 What procedures do you use to control the calibration process, whether this is carried out in-house or sub-contracted?

9 What calibration records do you keep?'

## Statistical techniques

1 Are statistical techniques used in your business?

2 If so, have you documented the methods used?

3 How do you ensure the individuals who use those techniques are trained and competent?

4 Are your methods based on sound, recognised statistical theory?

## Handling, storage, packaging, preservation and delivery

1 How do you protect products or services from damage or corruption during handling?

2 How are movements between processes controlled to prevent errors?

3 Are storage areas secure?

**4** Are items protected and preserved during storage from damage, deterioration, loss or incorrect identification?

**5** Are the stores receipt and issuing procedures adequate to prevent the mixing of different products?

**6** Is there a system to ensure stock is regularly checked to detect any deterioration?

**7** What provisions do you make to ensure items with a 'shelf life' are not used after their expiry date?

**8** What procedures exist to ensure items are adequately packed and identified to prevent damage or loss during delivery?

**9** How do you control the delivery process to ensure the correct goods and services are delivered, on time, undamaged to the correct location?

### Purchaser supplied product

**1** How would you recognise customer supplied items on receipt at your premises?

**2** How would you verify these items for damage and conformance to requirements on receipt?

**3** How are the items identified to ensure they are used as required by your agreement with the customer?

**4** How are items identified and stored to prevent loss, damage or incorrect use?

**5** What happens if a non-conformance arises? How is the customer informed?

## 10

# Corrective and preventive action

■ **Prevention is better than cure**

■ **Corrective action systems constantly improve performance**

■ **Features of an effective corrective action system**

■ **Controlling non-conforming products and services to prevent inadvertent use**

■ **Checklist**

## Prevention is better than cure

It has always been implicit within ISO9000 that simply fixing what has gone wrong is not a satisfactory way of working; what is required is effective action to prevent recurrence. ISO9000 1994 reinforces this perception by adding the need for preventive action to the Standard requirement; preventive action is now given equal importance to corrective action.

Many organisations waste as much as 25 per cent of their time finding and fixing errors because they do not produce conforming output first time round. There are three key reasons why a process may not produce conforming output:

(i)   the output requirements are not understood, defined and agreed;

(ii)  the process is not capable of meeting the requirements; or

> Note: ISO9001 defines the requirements for non-conformance and for corrective and preventive action in paragraphs 4.13 and 4.14.

(iii) the process is not being controlled to ensure it produces only conforming output.

Many businesses accept that they will produce non-conforming product. They introduce elaborate test or inspection procedures to try and ensure none of their defective products or services reach their customers. This is not an efficient way to run a business:

- you will not identify every non-conforming product or service. You will, therefore, sometimes fail to meet the requirements of your customers

- it is very costly to test, inspect and rework products or services

- it is time consuming. Test and inspection will introduce delays into your production process

- you may introduce errors. You may damage integrated circuits, scratch paint on cars, put papers back in the wrong file or drop sensitive equipment

118

- you run the risk of removing ownership for conformance from those responsible for the process. They may be encouraged to believe it does not matter what they do. Any errors will be picked up and corrected later.

This is not the route to success. An effective Quality Management System is based on the concept of controlling processes and preventing errors arising. The steps in operating an effective prevention system are:

(i)   ensure you understand the processes within your business;

(ii)  set up each process so it is 'in control'. This requires management of the parameters that control the process to ensure that output conforms to requirements;

(iii) ensure the process owners monitor the key characteristics of the process. The purpose is to monitor trends and introduce corrective actions before the process drifts out of control and produces non-conforming output; and

(iv)  if non-conformances are identified the following steps should be taken immediately:

- ensure the non-conforming products/services are not inadvertently used, installed or delivered

- ensure the causes of non-conformance are fully investigated and removed. The objective here is to ensure the error will not recur. This is known as Corrective and Preventive Action.

The presence of errors must always be treated seriously since it may reveal a significant breakdown in your system and may mean you can no longer have confidence in your ability to produce only conforming products and services. Some Japanese manufacturers place such importance on Quality that they allow anyone who identifies non-conforming product to halt the production line until the cause of the error has been identified and eliminated.

# Corrective and preventive action systems constantly improve performance

Investigating the root causes of errors and implementing effective preventive actions is the cornerstone of an effective Quality Management System. Merely fixing errors is not adequate. A system must be established which ensures they are eliminated, not just for today, but for ever. There are three stages in an effective corrective action system:

119

(i)   short-term fix: this is the immediate fix for an identified error;

(ii)  the cure: investigate the root cause of the errors and eliminate them; and

(iii) prevention of errors: identify potential causes of error by analysing data to detect trends which, if allowed to continue without intervention, would result in errors. Data sources can include customer complaints, warranty reports, system audits and yield reports. ISO9000 focuses attention on the analysis of customer complaints, as this reveals instances where the system has broken down to such an extent that a customer has received a non-conforming product or service.

Given the emphasis in ISO9000 on developing a QMS focused on meeting customer requirements, the QMS must ensure that all customer complaints are recorded, investigated thoroughly, effective actions taken to resolve the problem and to prevent recurrence and that the customer is kept informed of the outcome.

The objective of all corrective action is to prevent errors occurring. This process improves your ability to meet your customers' requirements and minimises the cost of non-conformance. An effective corrective action system requires a logical and systematic approach:

(i)   analyse the processes so you understand how they operate. This is frequently achieved by flow charting the process and defining process inputs, controls and outputs;

(ii) monitor processes so you detect errors and identify trends which might give rise to errors;

(iii) investigate all the potential causes of the problem. A number of problem solving techniques may be applied here, including brainstorming, cause and effect diagrams and voting, weighting and experimentation. The objective is to identify the most likely root cause of the problem;

(iv) take actions to eliminate the root cause of the problem;

(v) monitor the effectiveness of the corrective action to ensure it really does eliminate the problem; and

(vi) record the actions taken.

The procedures you use to identify the root cause of problems, implement, monitor and record corrective actions should be documented. This system should cover corrective actions taken when non-conformances are identified as well as the analysis of trends and consequent intervention to prevent errors occurring.

Many companies already operate corrective action systems but these are often ineffective for a number of reasons. The actions taken when problems have been identified are often not really preventive actions. They may fix today's problem but often do not introduce the long-term improvements necessary to prevent the problem recurring in the future. The typical approach to resolving problems in many companies is to form a team of managers and supervisors. These teams are formed on an *ad hoc* basis and meet to try and resolve significant problems as they are identified. Using only managers and supervisors in these teams may restrict their ability to solve problems. It is important to involve people in these teams who do the job on a day-to-day basis. They will understand their processes in detail and will understand the impact of different courses of action on those processes.

# Features of an effective corrective and preventive action system

To be effective it is important that corrective actions are properly planned and implemented. They will then be able to eliminate the problems once and for all. The following features typically need to be present in order for a corrective action system to be effective:

(i) an effective mechanism should exist to identify errors or adverse trends as they arise;

(ii) once a problem has been identified it is important to involve people concerned with the problem in investigating the causes of error and developing corrective actions;

(iii) someone within each group, frequently the supervisor, needs to have some knowledge of problem solving methods;

(iv) the team chairman should have some understanding of team dynamics to ensure effective team working. Teams bring together representatives from all the functions affected by the problem. This helps to ensure effective corrective actions are identified. It also helps improve the interfaces between departments;

(v) corrective actions should be carefully assessed to ensure they are the most effective means of eliminating the problem once and for all. The results of corrective actions should be monitored to ensure they achieve the objectives set for them; and

vi) management must demonstrate their commitment by taking an effective interest in the progress made by problem solving teams.

The basis for all effective corrective action systems is a system of records. This should include:

■ records of non-conformance to enable you to investigate the root causes of problems and prevent the recurrence of errors

■ records of performance to enable you to analyse trends to prevent errors occurring in the first place

121

# Controlling non-conforming products or services to prevent inadvertent use

If you identify instances of non-conforming products or services you should ensure they are not inadvertantly used, installed or delivered. An effective Quality Management System should address the following key points:

■ identification of suspect products and services

- documentation
- review and disposal
- notification of actions required.

## IDENTIFICATION

Suspect products and services should be labelled in such a way that their status is identifiable to any individual who might otherwise carry out further work on them, or deliver them to a customer. For example, if a draft contract prepared for a customer is found to contain errors it is important that the method of identification prevents it being typed up, or delivered.

The system should also ensure that when a non-conformance is found, other products or services which may have followed the same process should be identified as suspect. For example if an individual in a hospital ward fails to follow precautions for segregating sharp material, such as scalpels or syringes, from other waste then all other bags of rubbish from the same department should be considered suspect. They should be identified as potentially non-conforming and await further investigation.

The means used to identify non-conforming material may vary greatly. The only requirement is that the means of identification should be clear and should stay in place until a decision is made about disposal. Where possible, non-conforming material should be physically segregated from conforming material.

The QMS should define the appropriate means of identifying non-conforming material and specify who is responsible for carrying out this identification.

## DOCUMENTATION

When an instance of non-conformance is identified, a full record should be generated for three reasons:

(i)   to enable an informed decision to be made on disposal;

(ii)  to enable the root cause of the non-conformance to be investigated and effective corrective actions introduced; and

(iii) to provide evidence that the QMS has been followed and is effective.

The documents should record the following details about the non-conforming material:

- the identity of the non-conforming product or service. This may be by referring to, for example, the part number and issue, the customer contract, the stage of work or the process and time of incident
- at what stage in the process the non-conformance was identified, and by whom. This helps identify other potentially non-conforming products and also helps when investigating the root cause of the problem
- the number of items affected and the extent of the non-conformance. This determines the size of the problem
- a full description of the non-conformance to enable sound decisions to be taken on the actions required, and to assist the investigation of root causes.

Having fully documented the non-conformance the same record can, if carefully designed, also be used to record:

- the immediate decision taken on disposal and the basis for that decision
- the results of the investigation to identify the root cause of the problem, together with the corrective action implemented to eliminate it.

The QMS should define the nature of these records and specify:

- what information should be recorded
- who is responsible for recording the information
- how the records should be stored.

123

## REVIEW AND DISPOSAL

All instances of non-conformance should be reviewed and a decision taken about what to do with the non-conforming products or services. The review should identify the impact of the non-conformance on safety, function, customer satisfaction, reliability and cost. This information can be used as a basis for reviewing alternative courses of action. There are generally four possible alternative courses of action:

- rework the product/service so it meets the requirements. In this case the method of rework and acceptance criteria should be documented
- accept the product as it is. This may mean accepting the deviation.

Here the deviation would need to be authorised by a concession, or by officially changing the requirement. Alternatively it may be found on further investigation that the product or service did indeed meet the requirements

- regrade the product or service for an alternative use. If an item is produced which is a slightly different colour to that required then this may have little impact on customer satisfaction and none on safety and reliability. In this case a decision might be made to regrade the items as seconds

- reject or scrap as unusable and un-reworkable. A non-conformance which has a major impact on safety may mean that the whole batch of output must be tested to identify defects. All non-conforming products would have to be reworked or scrapped. In the most serious cases this could even involve a complete recall of all products in the field.

It is important that any decisions are soundly based on factual data, and made by individuals with the skills and experience necessary to equip them to make such decisions. The requirements of your customers are paramount during this decision-making process. There may even be a requirement to involve your customers in the process. For example, if a customer requires a new service to be launched on a given day and you identify a non-conformance, then you would expect to involve your customer in the decision on the appropriate action to take.

Your QMS should define:

- who is involved in the review process
- what criteria are to be used as the basis for decisions
- what data is required to make a decision
- how is the decision recorded
- how is the customer involved in the decision where this is a requirement.


## NOTIFICATION

You should ensure you that you are informed of any instances of non-conformance either during the production process or after delivery to enable effective actions to be taken. Any errors may indicate a failure in your QMS and need to be investigated.

For example, if an error is found during field service, it may be necessary to stop all shipments of that item pending further investigation. The system for notification should define who is required to be notified, how notification takes place and who is responsible for notification.

## CHECKLIST: CORRECTIVE ACTION

**1** Does your system identify who is responsible for identifying non-conforming products and services?

**2** How are non-conforming products identified? Is the method conspicuous and adequate? Is non-conforming product segregated? If not then what are the reasons?

**3** Does the system adequately identify what records need to be kept to record an incidence of non-conformance, together with the subsequent actions taken?

**4** Who is responsible for disposal decisions? What criteria are used as a basis for these decisions? What records are required to be kept to support these decisions?

**5** How is the customer involved or informed of these decisions, where this is a requirement?

**6** When rework takes place, does your system require rework methods and acceptance criteria to be defined?

**7** What system have you implemented to inform all relevant functions of non-conformances and actions required?

**8** Who is responsible for initiating the investigation into the root causes of any non-conformance and implementing corrective actions? Does this system adequately ensure that all customer complaints are fully investigated?

**9** How do you investigate the root causes of any non-conformance? How do you assess corrective actions before implementation?

**10** What trend analysis is carried out to detect potential non-conformances before they arise? What data is analysed, by whom, how often and how is it analysed?

**11** How do you verify that any corrective action implemented is effective and removes the root cause of the error?

**12** What records are kept of the investigation and the actions taken?

**13** When investigation shows that changes are required to processes or procedures how are these actioned?

# Maintaining an effective Quality Management System

- ■ Maintaining an effective Quality Management System
- ■ Benefiting from internal quality system audits
- ■ Benefiting from external audits
- ■ Benefiting from management review
- ■ Ensuring your employees have the skills required to develop your business
- ■ Checklist

## Maintaining an effective Quality Management System

A Quality Management System will only be effective if management ensures it is understood and implemented throughout the organisation and that it evolves so it continues to meet the needs of the business. Management may monitor their QMS and identify opportunities for improvement using three principal methods:

> Note: ISO9001 defines the requirements for maintaining the Quality System in paragraph 4.1, 4.17 and 4.18.

(i)   Quality System audits;

(ii)  management reviews; and

(iii) analysis of the people skills within the organisation.

# Benefiting from internal Quality System Audits

Internal Quality System Audits verify that activities are carried out in accordance with the QMS, and that the QMS continues to meet the needs of the business and the requirements of ISO9000. Effective audits by competent auditors which are taken seriously by management are the key to ensuring that your Quality Management System remains 'alive' and delivers the full benefits for your business.

There are two principal objectives of a Quality System Audit:

- to ensure the QMS, as documented, meets the requirements of ISO9000. Many businesses blindly assume that this is so. However, this may well not be true. There is little point in ensuring that everyone is following a QMS if it does not meet the requirements of ISO9000

- to ensure that the QMS is understood and followed by everyone.

They also provide one of the best opportunities for analysing your QMS to identify ways in which it can be improved. You might identify procedures which enable you to control your business better. Alternatively you might identify existing inspection and test activities which could be replaced by improved control of the underlying process.

Internal quality audits are taken very seriously by the certification bodies during external audits. The effectiveness of the internal auditing system usually provides a barometer of how committed the organisation is to its Quality Management System. Well-performed audits with a rapid response to deficiencies generally indicate an effective and widely-respected QMS which is actively working to improve business performance.

An ineffective QMS usually results in Quality System Audits which are poorly carried out and whose results are largely ignored by the organisation. As a consequence this is usually one of the areas subject to close scrutiny by external auditors.

Your QMS should define the procedures you use for carrying out Quality System Audits. This documented system should cover the following points:

- responsibility
- scheduling
- planning
- execution
- reporting
- corrective actions.

## RESPONSIBILITY

Your QMS should define who is responsible for carrying out audits. Although the Standard does not define who should be responsible for audits, it states that they need to be qualified, competent, and independent of the area being audited. Your QMS must document how you fulfil this requirement. Auditors require a number of important skills:

(i)   a thorough understanding of the requirements of ISO9000 and the ability to determine whether an activity, as presented, meets those requirements;

(ii)  an understanding of how to plan an audit, how to follow an audit trail and how to gather objective evidence;

(iii) the ability to think creatively to identify potential problems in the existing system, or to identify possible improvements to the existing system;

(iv)  the ability to communicate sensitively with a wide range of individuals. The audit process can give rise to stress in some people. The auditor should work to minimise this;

(v)   the ability to record events clearly and unambiguously; and

(vi)  the ability to distinguish important issues and focus on them.

It is a requirement of ISO9000 that the organisation should provide adequate, trained personnel to carry out quality audits. Although the Standard does not specify the training required, there are a number of system auditing courses available; some auditor training or extensive experience would be necessary to develop the skills and knowledge required to carry out effective audits. It is the organisation's responsibility to assess and fulfil any auditor training needs.

## SCHEDULING

Audits should be systematic and carried out in accordance with a preplanned schedule. They should not just be carried out in response to problems arising. Your QMS should therefore define how the audit schedule is put together; who is responsible for defining it, what the criteria are for determining the areas/activities for audit and how the schedule is recorded.

The schedule should ensure that all the applicable requirements of ISO9000 are thoroughly audited over a suitable timeframe. The Standard does not define the length of this timeframe, although many organisations use a period of one year. The planned frequency of auditing any particular requirement or function depends on how critical it is in ensuring conformance to requirements and whether any problems are known to exist.

Organisations generally carry out audits in one of two ways:

- they schedule each department for audit and then audit all the ISO9000 requirements which apply to that department (functional audit)
- they schedule all the ISO9000 requirements for audit and then audit all the departments to which that requirement applies (requirements audit).

Functional audits are generally easier to schedule and carry out since only one department is audited at a time and the boundaries are clear cut, but they have a number of disadvantages:

(i)   each department is audited infrequently and so the impact of changes may not be identified rapidly;

(ii)  the tendency is to focus on major requirements in each department. At the end of the schedule it may be found that some of the more minor, although still important, requirements have not been audited thoroughly;

(iii) it is more difficult to see system deficiencies against any one requirement which has an impact on a number of departments. A single deficiency may be recorded against a requirement in a number of departments. An inexperienced auditor may not link these together although they might indicate a serious system deficiency; and

(iv) processes frequently cross departmental boundaries so it can be difficult to assess the impact of any given activity on the operation of the whole process.

Requirements auditing enables system deficiencies to be identified more easily as the same requirement is audited across the business. However, it is generally more difficult to plan and carry out requirements audits since a number of departments are involved. Also, because many of the requirements interlink, it is often difficult to restrict an audit trail to just one requirement. One way to overcome this is to link together closely-related requirements and audit them at the same time.

You should design a system which minimises the impact of the above disadvantages within your organisation. The method you select should be documented.

131

When constructing your audit schedule it is useful to use the following headings:

- the function(s) to be audited
- the ISO9000 requirement(s) covered
- the planned date for the audit
- when the audit was carried out
- the number of deficiencies raised
- the date corrective actions were implemented
- the date the audit was closed.

In this way it is possible to ensure that all functions and requirements have been audited during the specified timeframe. It is important to have a system which tracks open audits until all corrective actions have been implemented and the audit can be closed off.

In addition to the scheduled audits, you may need to carry out additional *ad hoc* audits in response to particular problems. Your system should describe how they are controlled. The same system should usually be followed for *ad hoc* audits as for scheduled audits. They are supplementary audits which contribute additional information on the general health of your QMS.

## PLANNING

It is important that audits are carried out systematically, consistently and comprehensively. Effective planning is the cornerstone of a good audit. This planning starts when the audit schedule is put together as this determines the overall scope of each audit. The plans for individual audits determine how the audit will be carried out within that scope. A competent, professional auditor would define a tailored plan for each audit. Each plan would be based on the results of past audits, the ISO9000 Standard, the procedures under review and details of any known problem areas. This ensures each audit takes a different slant rather than being a re-run of the previous audit. This approach enables the auditor to:

- identify problem areas which might be missed by a less well planned audit

- identify opportunities for improving control of business processes.

However, many organisations favour the use of audit checklists, and this seems to be encouraged by the registration bodies. A checklist can be a useful baseline or *aide-memoire* to guide the auditor. If, however, they are used as a 'tick list' they can lead to superficial, routine audits, which focus on trivial issues and fail to recognise more serious system deficiencies. It can, therefore, severely restrict an auditor's ability to identify opportunities for improvement to the QMS. Effective auditing is a skilled task requiring an understanding of ISO9000 and the rigorous, informed pursuit of an audit trail to produce the most beneficial results. A checklist can be an addition to the skills of a good auditor, but it cannot be a substitute for them!

Your QMS should document the procedures you use for audit planning.

## EXECUTION

The purpose of the audit is to seek objective evidence that the QMS is adequate, documented, understood and followed. Objective evidence is provided by documents, records and testing the understanding of individual process operators. An auditor has two main sources from which to gather evidence. Talking to individuals provides evidence that they understand and follow the QMS. Examining records provides evidence that the QMS has been followed.

Most audits make use of evidence from both these sources to provide an overall picture of the effectiveness of the QMS. The audit plan defines how the audit will be performed. The skill and experience of the auditor ensures that:

- the plan is followed during the audit
- open-ended questions are asked to check operator understanding of the system
- an audit trail is followed to determine the full extent of any problem identified
- the audit focuses on important issues as these become evident during the course of the audit
- if a deficiency is found, the auditor can assess if this is actually an opportunity to improve the QMS.

## REPORTING

A report should be issued following each audit. This should be an accurate summary of the audit events and findings. It is useful to give each audit a unique reference number. To ensure consistency in reporting, the audit procedure should define the information required within your audit reports. A typical audit report would cover the following:

133

- auditor – who carried out the audit and when
- scope – what was audited, the areas and the requirements
- summary – how the audit was carried out, what was audited (may refer to audit plan), summary of events
- deficiencies – details of instances when the requirements were not met
- conclusions – conclusions on the overall audit. This also provides an opportunity for the auditor to identify potential improvements to the QMS.

## CORRECTIVE ACTION

For audits to be effective it is important that any deficiencies found are brought to management attention and acted upon rapidly. The reporting of audit deficiencies, implementation of corrective actions and follow up must therefore be documented as part of the audit procedure. Often, in addition to the audit report, deficiencies are documented and referenced individually so they can be circulated as required and used to stimulate corrective action. A well designed audit deficiency report can detail the deficiency found and can also be used to record details of the corrective action implemented and the follow-up to ensure the corrective action was effective. The audit deficiency report should detail the following:

- report number
- auditor
- date of audit
- function and requirement audited
- deficiency found
- person responsible for corrective action
- proposed corrective action
- date for completion of corrective action
- verification by auditor of the effectiveness of the corrective action.

The procedure should describe how deficiencies are documented, how they are brought to the attention of management in the area where the deficiency occurred, how the corrective action taken is recorded and how its effectiveness is verified. It is the responsibility of the auditor to bring deficiencies to the attention of management. It is then the responsibility of the appropriate manager to implement the necessary corrective action.

An example of an audit procedure, together with an audit report and an audit deficiency record are provided in Appendices 4, 6 and 7.

# Benefiting from external audits

External audits are carried out either by a third-party assessing body, or sometimes by a customer. These are really not a great deal different from your own internal audits and will be carried out in a very similar way. They may look at a small number of elements of ISO9000 (a surveillance visit). This would be almost identical to your own audits. Alternatively, they may look at the QMS in its entirety (an assessment visit). This is like a series of internal audits carried out by a small team of auditors.

The best way to prepare for external audits is to ensure you have a rigorous and effective internal audit system. This will ensure the following:

(i) you have confidence in your QMS; you know it is working effectively and have nothing to fear. There are no hidden surprises;

(ii) people within your organisation are familiar and comfortable with audits. They will know what sort of questions are asked and how to react; and

(iii) the external auditor will have greater confidence in your QMS.

If your organisation believes in its QMS, it will see auditing as a positive monitoring of the health of that QMS. An external audit is just another valuable independent view of the QMS. It is not a threat.

It is also important to remember that in the case of an independent third-party audit all deficiencies will be discussed with you by the auditor. The auditor can only raise a deficiency if he can demonstrate that your QMS fails to meet one of the requirements of ISO9000. He cannot raise a deficiency just because he has a different view of how things should be done. If you do not agree with a deficiency then discuss your view with the assessor. It is, however, not possible to do this if your organisation does not itself understand the ISO9000 requirements!

135

# Benefiting from management review

A system audit is designed to test the operation of specific procedures and processes in the Quality Management System. The objective of a system audit is to assess whether or not the QMS meets the requirements of ISO9000, is understood and is implemented.

Management reviews take a look at the effectiveness of the QMS to meet the long-term requirements of the business. The purpose of the management review is for the most senior managers of the organisation to periodically look at their Quality Policy and Quality System to review its effectiveness; determine whether any changes are required; and to re-affirm their commitment to its aims and objectives. A review may take place annually, as part of the business planning process. Management reviews consider data from a variety of sources to determine whether the QMS meets the needs of:

■ the customers

■ the business, as described in the Quality Policy

- the Quality Standard requirements.

Data may be gathered from a number of sources for management review. Typical sources might include:

- internal audit results
- external audit results
- customer complaints
- warranty statistics
- supplier performance
- non-conformance reports
- performance measures – process yield, turnaround times, error levels
- changes within the business
- changes in the Standards
- quality costs.

The procedure used to carry out and record management reviews needs to be documented and should cover:

- who is involved
- frequency
- what criteria are used
- how is the review carried out and recorded
- how are corrective actions recorded (responsibilities, timescales and follow-up).

Following a management review a formal record should be produced recording what took place; any changes required; and recording senior management on-going commitment to the Quality System and to the Quality Policy.

# Ensuring your employees have the skills required to develop your business

The QMS defines how business processes are to be operated. These processes can only be operated as described if the individuals have sufficient skill, knowledge and experience. An important element in the QMS is therefore the analysis and fulfilment of training needs. ISO9000 requires that a system exists to regularly monitor the skills required to operate the business and ensure these skills exist within the workforce. The system must therefore include:

(i)   a means of assessing the skills required by the business. This is often achieved by using job specifications to define the skills required for a particular job;

(ii)  a means of assessing the skills base of the workforce. This is often achieved by using an appraisal system to identify training needs; and

(iii) a means of demonstrating that training needs have been met. This is often achieved by training records.

Training can be provided in any form suitable to fulfil the need and may include:

- external training courses
- internal training courses
- correspondence courses
- on the job training.

The form of training is not important. What is important is that it adequately fulfils an identified need, and a record is kept of the training carried out.

## CHECKLIST: MONITORING AN EFFECTIVE QUALITY MANAGEMENT SYSTEM

### Quality System Audit

1 Have you determined who is responsible for carrying out Quality System Audits? How will you ensure that this person (people) is qualified, competent and independent of the area audited?

2 What process do you follow for scheduling audits? How do you deal with *ad hoc* audits?

3 What process is followed when planning and conducting audits?

4 How do you control the reporting of audits?

5 How do you ensure that the appropriate managers are informed of audit deficiencies and take appropriate corrective action? How do you ensure the effectiveness of the corrective action?

### Management review

1 Have you produced a document defining how, when and who is involved in management review?

2 Have you defined the data on which management judges the effectiveness of the QMS?

3 What records of management review are maintained?

4 How are corrective actions documented, implemented and followed up? Are these methods all documented?

5 Does the review process ensure that senior management formally review the Quality Policy?

### Training review

1 How do you identify the skills required to perform the activities of your business?

2 What system do you use to identify training needs, both specific task-related training and quality awareness training?

**3** How do you fulfil any training needs identified?

**4** What records do you keep to provide evidence that training needs have been identified and appropriate training provided?

# Document control

- **Controlling the documentation**
- **Control of format**
- **Issuing documents**
- **Controlling changes to documents**
- **Keeping records**
- **Checklist**

## Controlling the documentation

Having determined the documentation you require to define your Quality Management System, you need to control it. Control of documents is required to ensure everyone operates a process in the same way, following the same instructions, and to ensure that procedures are defined, approved and understood.

Any document which has an impact on the Quality of your products or services must be controlled. There are four key elements in any system of effective document control:

(i)   document format;

(ii)  authorisation of documents;

(iii) issue and withdrawal procedures; and

(iv)  changes to documents.

All Quality-related documents need to be controlled. These may include the Quality Manual, procedures, work instructions, specifications or

Note: ISO9001 defines the requirements for document control and records in paragraph 4.5.

drawings. This covers external documents, for example specifications, handbooks, training material, in addition to documents generated internally.

# Control of format

The system to control the format of documentation should address the following issues:

- reference
- issue status
- authorisation
- style and content.

## REFERENCE

142

A document can only be controlled if it can be uniquely identified so everyone knows unambiguously that they are referring to the same document. This reduces the risk of confusion and errors amongst users. Using document titles is not usually adequate as a number of documents may have similar titles. The allocation of a unique, simple number is an effective means of identifying documents. This ensures that when a document is referred to, everyone will understand the reference. Systems may vary from a simple sequential numbering of documents, to more complex systems using special suffixes or prefixes to provide information on the type of document, or the department responsible for generating it. Different systems may be appropriate to different organisations depending on the size and complexity of the documentation requirements.

## ISSUE STATUS

All documents must be capable of being changed if they are to continue to reflect the needs of an evolving business. Accordingly, there must be some means of distinguishing between different versions of the same document. Everyone must work a given process in the same way, following the same instructions. This can only be achieved if they work to the same version of the document. Since a new version of a document may fundamentally change the way a process is operated, it is essential that different versions of the same basic document can be identified. This may be achieved by associating an issue status with the document number. These two together uniquely identify the document. The issue status may take the form of a letter or number which is incrementally increased with each new issue of the document, for example issue A, followed by issue B and C; or issue 01 followed by issue 02 and 03.

## AUTHORISATION

Before a document can be released it must be authorised. This can only be undertaken by designated individuals with the required skills to make the final decision as to how a process should operate. Different individuals will almost certainly be responsible for authorising changes to different documents.

The most appropriate place to define who has authority to release documents is usually within each procedure. The overall document control procedure should define how the authorising individuals or functions are selected.

143

Each procedure should describe the authority required before release of the document and that, once reviewed, approval is signified on the document, usually via a signature.

## STYLE AND CONTENT

Determining a standard format and contents for documents has three significant benefits:

(i)   it makes documents easier for individuals to follow and use as the subject matter always appears in the same way. This should reduce the risk of errors;

(ii)  the use of a standard document format ensures that essential elements are considered. For procedures the format should include all the common ISO9000 requirements. If any requirements are omitted the user may infer that they have been considered and purposely left out as inappropriate. They will not just have been overlooked. Standard drawing sheets may be used to control and define the way drawings should be laid out, and specify standard information required on the drawing; and

(iii) in order to facilitate updates, documents are usually issued either loose or within a file. It is important to be able to verify that all the pages are included and are in the correct order. It is possible for pages to go missing. If this remains undetected by the user there is a danger that the process could be operated incorrectly. A simple way of overcoming this problem is to ensure each page is numbered within an overall number sequence. Each page could be numbered sequentially as '1 of $n$', '2 of $n$', '3 of $n$' and so forth, where $n$ is the total number of pages within the document.

# Issuing documents

To ensure your products and services meet the requirements of your customers, you must ensure everyone operates the procedures as planned. This can only be achieved if the operating requirements have been documented, and the same version of these documents is available to everyone who needs to use them. Your Quality Management System should define:

144

(i)  who should receive a copy of each document. Here a balance needs to be struck between restricting the number of documents issued to reduce the risk of errors in the issuing mechanism; and the need to ensure everyone has access to the documents they need to operate their processes with minimum error. In some businesses it may be acceptable to issue just one set of documents to a given work area and then ensure everyone is aware of the documents, what is in them, where they are and the importance of understanding their contents. This can be achieved through both verbal and written communication. In other businesses it may be necessary to issue each procedure to everyone involved in that process;

(ii)  how new documents are issued and obsolete documents withdrawn. It is important to avoid the risk of obsolete documents being available. The return of withdrawn documents when issuing new ones is quite an effective control. This can provide assurance that all old documents have been withdrawn. This process may be:

- centralised, so all documents are issued by one central body. This has the advantage that one area is responsible for all issues, so ensuring a consistent approach. This may be appropriate for organisations with a library, a drawing office, or an administration office. It can, however, produce a heavy burden for one individual in organisations that do not have these facilities.

- alternatively, responsibility for the issue of each document may be devolved to the major function responsible for its authorisation. This has the advantage that the workload is spread and each function accepts responsibility for its own documents. However, it does mean that the issue process becomes fragmented and potentially less consistent; and

(iii) a mechanism for identifying which issue of a document is current at any given time. One common question asked by an assessor is 'how do you know that you are working to the correct version of a document?' A master list of all documents and their revision status at any given time is frequently essential. Obviously, the more you devolve control for individual documents, the more master lists you will require. This document may be made available to individuals so they are able to ensure their documentation is current before use. Alternatively, the issue mechanism may be sufficiently robust so individuals can rely on their version being current. This is an area where many organisations fail at assessment since there is a great potential for error. The principal means of minimising the risk of failure are:

- minimise the number of documents in the QMS

- minimise the number of copies issued of any document, whilst ensuring individuals are aware of their contents

- design a simple and robust issuing mechanism

- audit the system regularly.

145

## Controlling changes to documents

Procedures evolve. It is always possible to think of ways to improve the way your business operates. Once a document has been generated and issued it will define the procedure your employees will be expected to follow. If you identify an improvement you will need to amend and reissue the procedure.

It is essential that you establish a system to ensure changes are implemented in a controlled way, so they are properly assessed and are implemented effectively. The key features of a system to control document changes are:

(i) details of the proposed change must be fully documented. This is the basis on which the assessment will be made;

(ii) the change must be reviewed thoroughly before acceptance;

(iii) all changes must be authorised. Where possible this should be the responsibility of the department, or individual responsible for the original document. This ensures continuity of approach and a greater understanding of the implications of the proposed change. However, it may not always be possible to achieve this, and so the system for change control should ensure sufficient information is provided to the person authorising the change to enable an informed decision to be made;

(iv) once a change has been incorporated within a document, it should be possible to identify details of the change. These details may be recorded in the document itself, or they may be recorded in another document. For drawings, the usual system is to record a brief description of the change on the drawing itself. Details of the change are recorded on a change note. The change note is referred to on the drawing. Similar procedures could be used for other documentation, including procedures, work instructions or technical manuals. An alternative approach is to include a list in the document of all previous issue numbers, together with a brief description of changes. This approach is often useful for procedures. A black line in the margin can be used to identify the text affected;

146

(v) long documents can become expensive to reissue when only a small number of minor changes have been made. This can be overcome by using an amendment system. Here individual pages of the document are changed and reissued rather than the whole document. This method can, however, make the documents less user friendly and less easy to control. You can avoid the need for an amendment system by ensuring all documents are concise. In this case it would be relatively easy and cost effective to reissue the whole document; and

(vi) it is important to keep a master list recording the current status and history of your documentation.

Having determined your policy for controlling documents you need to ensure that this system is itself documented. An example of a procedure used within a sales and marketing organisation to control its procedural documentation is provided in Appendix 3.

# Keeping records

If you want to control your business you must ensure that the procedures you define are, in fact, operated. You need to ensure, for example, contracts are reviewed, tests are carried out and quality audits have been completed. You will therefore need to keep records to demonstrate achievement of the Quality objectives. There are many types of record which should be kept to demonstrate the effective operation of your Quality Management System. These include:

- contract review records
- design review and test records
- inspection and test records
- calibration records
- records of non-conforming products or services, including customer complaints
- corrective action records
- audit reports
- management review minutes
- training records.

The format of these records is important. If you define records which are user friendly (a checklist against which to record a contract review or a standard audit report format) you will find they are used with some enthusiasm. It is important that you involve each process operator in defining what needs to be recorded for their process and the format of the record.

ISO9000 requires that evidence is kept to demonstrate that all the requirements have been met. Your QMS should therefore ensure each procedure defines the records required to demonstrate it has been followed. These records may need to be referred to long after they were generated. When defining your record system you should ensure the records:

- identify key details
- are legible and incorruptible
- are retrievable
- are disposed of in a controlled way.

147

## IDENTIFICATION

It should be possible to identify the product, service or event to which each record applies, and answer the following key questions:

- who was involved in the process?
- what was the subject of the record? What happened? What decision was taken?
- when did the event occur?
- where did the event occur?
- what was the basis for the decision? This may refer to a specific inspection procedure, or other documents if necessary.

Not all this information will be appropriate in every type of record, but it should be considered.

## LEGIBLE AND INCORRUPTIBLE

It must be possible for anyone else to be able to read the record in a meaningful way long after the recorded event. The record should remain readable throughout its storage period. It is important to consider storage conditions and storage media to ensure this. The records should be incorruptible and should not be subject to amendment. This is frequently achieved by restricting access to records.

## RETRIEVABLE

Records should be accessible during the storage period. You should consider where they are stored and how they are filed (for example by date order, record number order or grouped by product). Bear in mind that records may well need to be accessed in a different order to that in which they were stored. Within a series of records stored in date order, you might want, for example, to access a specific product record. You may therefore need a catalogue summarising the nature of the records and where they are stored.

## DISPOSAL

It is important that records are disposed of in a controlled way at the end of the storage period. It is important to define:

- how you identify records for disposal

- who authorises disposal.

The documentation of the record control system can be prepared in one of two ways, depending on the nature of your business and the types of records concerned:

- each individual procedure can define the record keeping requirements
- it may be preferable to generate an overall document defining the record keeping requirements common to all records, including retention time, storage media, storage responsibilities, disposal authorisation. Individual procedures could then just contain details of the specific records they require.

## Electronic records

Today, many transactions are carried out on computers and many records are held as computer files. In this instance records, including identification, legibility, incorruptibility, retrievability and disposal will be determined by the systems and processes of the computer systems organisation. It is, therefore, essential that the processes within this department are documented as part of your QMS since they have a significant impact on your ability to meet customer requirements. When documenting these processes, the following need to be considered:

149

(i) how is systems configuration controlled to ensure the system is maintainable?

(ii) when a system is networked, how is the network documented to ensure faults and problems can be traced rapidly and knock-on effects identified?

(iii) how is access to the system controlled to prevent corruption of data?

(iv) what is the process for carrying out data back-ups to prevent loss of data?

(v) what storage procedures are in place to ensure the long-term safe storage of data?

(vi) how are changes made to the systems in operation; who can make changes and what controls are in place? This may cover the purchase or design of new applications.

---

### CHECKLIST: DOCUMENT CONTROL

**1** Have you defined the QMS-related documents which need to be controlled?

**2** Has a document numbering system been established for unique numbers and issue status?

**3** Have you identified the criteria for establishing approval authorities?

**4** Have you identified the personnel authorised to approve each type of document? Where a procedure applies to more than one function has provision been made for review by all relevant parties?

**5** Does each document provide for recording the identities of the originator/approver(s)?

**6** Have you defined the standard style/content/pagination method for each document?

**7** Have you established who needs to be copied with each document?

**8** Have you established a system for the removal of obsolete documents?

**9** Do you maintain an up-to-date master register recording the status of all documents?

**10** How is the master register updated and how is the list made available to users (if required)?

**11** Does your change control system ensure that the original approvers of documents review changes?

**12** Where the above is not possible, how does your system ensure that sufficient information is made available to enable an informed decision to be made?

**13** Have you made provision on the document for the approver to authorise the change?

**14** How do you identify changes to a document?

**15** Have the systems identified above themselves been documented?

**16** Does you system cover externally generated, as well as internal, documents?

## Records

**1** Have you identified all the records necessary to demonstrate conformance with the Quality Management System?

**2** Have you ensured that the data in the records is identifiable with a specific product/service/event?

**3** What are the periods of storage and who is responsible for storage documented for each type of record? Have you defined where records are to be kept? Is access to stored records restricted?

**4** Are format conditions and media adequate?

**5** What system have you established to enable records to be retrieved?

**6** Are disposal methods and authorities defined?

**7** Have you included periodic reviews of records in storage as part of your audit system?

**8** Where eletronic records are involved, have you documented the computer systems processes?

# Appendices

■

## INTRODUCTION

The appendices include examples of quality documents designed for the Alpha Group. They illustrate the key features of documents used to ensure consistent product and service quality and to address the requirements of ISO9000 for a range of organisations. Most of the documents are drawn from the UK sub-group:

(i)   Omega International designs and manufactures instruments for the worldwide market; and

(ii)  Omega UK Ltd provides UK sales, marketing, support and training.

The documents provided in the appendices are as follows:

Appendix 1:  An introduction to the requirements of ISO9001.

Appendix 2:  The Quality Manual produced for Omega UK Ltd. This addresses the requirements of ISO9001 for a sales, distribution, support and training organisation.

Appendix 3:  A procedure describing how Omega UK Ltd controls its procedures.

Appendix 4:  A procedure describing how Omega UK Ltd controls the audit and management review of its Quality Management system.

Appendix 5:  A procedure describing how Omega UK Ltd carries out business planning.

Appendix 6:  A report on an audit of the design control procedures within the training department of Omega UK Ltd.

Appendix 7:  A report on an audit of the product handling activity for Omega International Ltd.

Appendix 8:  The Quality Policy of The Alpha Group.

Appendix 9:  Organisation charts for The Alpha Group:
9A  The Alpha Group
9B  Omega UK Ltd – Management structure chart

Appendix 10: A job description for the Training Director of Omega UK Ltd.

Appendix 11: A list of the accredited third party assessing bodies in the UK.

154

# Appendix 1

## SUMMARY OF THE CONTENTS OF BS EN ISO9001 1994

This section describes in outline the key requirements in each of the paragraphs of ISO9001 1994. It is designed to enable senior management to make an informed judgement about what is required to implement an effective QMS. A detailed description of how to implement an effective QMS to meet each of the requirements is given in Chapters 4 to 12.

## 1. QUALITY POLICY

To ensure Quality is taken seriously by all employees in an organisation, senior management should define and publish the company's Quality Policy. This defines the quality objectives of the business and helps demonstrate the commitment of senior management to Quality. Senior managers are then responsible for ensuring this policy is understood and implemented throughout the company. The Quality Policy must be relevant to the supplier's organisational goals and the expectations and needs of its customers.

## 2. ORGANISATION

The role and responsibilities of all functions which affect product or service quality should be defined. This is usually achieved by means of an organisation chart and job specifications. The company should identify the test, inspection and other monitoring activities required to assure product or service quality and ensure sufficient, trained personnel are available to carry them out.

A manager should be nominated and given the necessary authority, resources and responsibility to ensure the QMS is implemented and maintained. The manager should have sufficient freedom to carry out this task without conflicting with his other responsibilities.

A system of Quality audit and management review procedures should be implemented to ensure the QMS continues to meet the requirements of ISO9001. Overall responsibility for the review of the Quality System lies with the Executive Management. Management review is to be carried out at defined intervals. This is discussed further in Section 18.

## 3. QUALITY SYSTEM

Having nominated a manager and defined the organisational structure to assure Quality, the company should design an appropriate Quality Management System. This system should be fully documented. The activities which the system should control are detailed in the remainder of the Standard.

### QMS documentation

A comprehensive set of documentation is required to describe appropriate procedures to control the quality of the products and services. The different types of documentation may be illustrated as a pyramid as shown in Fig A.1.

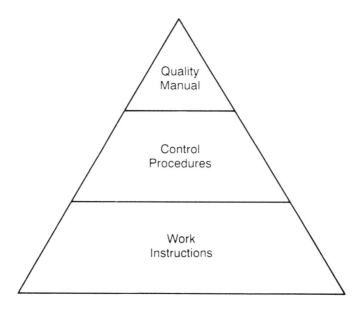

**Fig. A.1  Pyramid of documentation**

The Quality manual describes how a company ensures conformance to ISO9001. It usually starts with a statement of the Quality Policy, and defines how this is put into practice by addressing each of the requirements of ISO9001. Detailed control procedures and other documents are referred to as appropriate. The manual is a formal declaration by the company of how it assures Quality, and forms a documented set of managerial instructions on Quality matters.

Control procedures define in detail the methods and controls adopted throughout the organisation to assure Quality. These procedures generally affect a number of people or departments, and frequently cover interfaces between functions. Individual work instructions are referred to where appropriate.

Work instructions define how to perform specific tasks or processes. They generally apply only to one task or to a small group of people, and might include specific inspection instructions, test specifications, drawings, planning instructions and calibration methods.

For example, consider the documentation defining how 'in-process testing' is controlled. The Quality Manual may describe the overall policy on testing. It may refer to a routing procedure describing how the process is controlled. The routing procedure may define who decides what testing is required for any item and how you ensure items follow this routing. The routing procedure may state that all testing is carried out in accordance with the appropriate test specification. The test specification describes the tests to apply and how to carry out these tests at different stages during manufacture.

157

Quality documentation is one of the keys to running an effective QMS. As a result, it is important to define how each level of documentation will be controlled (see paragraph 6). It is also important to understand the relationship between documents to ensure any changes take account of all the knock-on effects which might occur.

The requirement to document the Quality system is modified by the statement that documented procedures should be consistent with the Standard and the range and detail of the procedures and instructions required depends on the complexity of the work, the methods used and the skills employed for any particular activity.

## 4. CONTRACT REVIEW

The QMS defines how an organisation assures the quality of the product or service it expects to provide. When accepting an order or contract to supply a product or service to a given specification, it is important to ensure the company is capable of meeting the specific requirements. All orders or contracts should, therefore, be reviewed before acceptance to ensure the requirements are capable of being met. Orders or contracts should not be accepted unless the company is capable of meeting the requirements. The following questions need to be asked at this stage:

- are the processes and equipment used capable of meeting the requirements?

- does the company have sufficient skilled personnel?

- are the methods currently used for testing, inspecting and monitoring output adequate to meet the requirements?

- are the equipment and methods currently used for taking measurements and testing capable of the required accuracy?

- does the company fully understand the acceptance criteria? All those items which determine whether or not the item meets the customer's requirements should be written down and fully understood. This includes a proper definition of any subjective judgements such as 'smooth finish', 'scratch-free', or 'blue'.

- are all the necessary processes (including design, production, inspection and test) compatible and capable of producing the product or service in accordance with requirements?

- do procedures exist to produce appropriate records?

158

A documented system should exist to ensure this review is undertaken before an order is accepted. The system should ensure the following points are checked:

(i)    the requirements are clearly stated in writing;

(ii)   any differences between the order and the original quotation/tender are resolved; and

(iii)  the company is capable of meeting the requirements.

It is usually possible to implement a fairly simple procedure to check points (i) and (ii) when standard or repeat orders are received. It may then be possible to restrict checks to identifying unusual features and ensuring these are fully documented before accepting the order. A more rigorous procedure should be implemented whenever new orders, non-standard orders, or special contracts are received. This will require a more detailed check against the above criteria. A documentary record should be kept to demonstrate that this review has taken place. For companies which do not usually produce standard items but work to specific contracts, the above points are often documented as part of a Quality plan prepared specifically for individual contracts.

The company is also required to document the procedure to be adopted when order/contract amendments are required.

## 5. DESIGN CONTROL

Procedures covering the following activities should be fully documented:

- planning
- design input
- design output
- design verification
- design validation
- design changes.

### *Planning*

The organisation of the design function should be documented so responsibility for each activity and interfaces between activities are defined. It is essential that everyone understands their role and responsibilities in the design process and their interface with other groups. The person responsible for each activity should have the necessary qualifications and sufficient resources to carry out the activity.

Procedures should specify how and when information is transmitted between groups. The timely flow of controlled and accurate information is essential to ensure the design process is carried out effectively and without errors in cases where a number of groups work on specific elements of complex designs.

### *Design input*

Design requirements may be received directly from external customers or from internal sources such as the marketing department. Before accepting a design requirement, the design department should review it to ensure it is sufficiently detailed to enable them to know what is expected from the design process.

### *Design output*

Output from the design process may consist of drawings and specifications supported by calculations, analyses, tests and reviews to demonstrate that the design conforms to the requirements. Design procedures should ensure that the design output:

(i) meets the input requirements. It is only possible to do this if the input requirements are adequately specified;

(ii)  contains instructions to define how conformance of the product or service can be verified during production;

(iii)  meets all the necessary regulatory requirements. The design process should ensure that all regulatory requirements are considered, not only those specified as part of the input requirements; and

(iv)  meets necessary safety standards. The design department should identify all parts of the design which are safety critical so they can be carefully monitored during the production process.

### Design verification

Procedures should exist to ensure the design output conforms in all regards to the input requirements. Design verification should be planned, performed and the results fully documented as part of the design process. A number of methods may be acceptable depending on circumstances. Typical methods include:

- holding design reviews
- undertaking tests
- carrying out checking calculations
- comparing the new design with similar, proven designs.

Typically, a combination of these methods might be adopted, although at least one design review must be carried out during the design process. The company should consider carefully which methods are most appropriate for any given design project. Unless a design is proven before it is released for production, it is likely that significant rectification costs and wasted time will arise during the production process.

### Design validation

This is additional to, and follows, successful design verification. The purpose of design validation is to ensure the performance of the design under actual conditions of use. Typically, design validation may include:

- prototype testing
- commissioning trials
- trial marketing of a product or service.

### Design changes

Whenever a change is made either during the design phase or to a

160

released design, the change should be proven, approved and communicated to everyone concerned in a controlled way. The procedures necessary to control design changes usually form part of the document control system.

## 6. DOCUMENT AND DATA CONTROL

An effective QMS ensures that all activities are carried out in a controlled way so that everyone knows what they are supposed to do. This requires documentation of how tasks should be performed. Because many processes are related and interdependent, it is important to ensure any change is implemented by everyone at the same time. This requires a system to ensure documents are controlled so that everyone who needs to use a document has easy access to it, and only the current version of a document is available at any time. This avoids confusion and mistakes.

Procedures should cover the origination and amendment of documents, detailing who holds the document; who may authorise changes; how documents are reissued; how obsolete documents are withdrawn; and a system for verifying the current version (perhaps using a master list). Key documents which need to be controlled include:

161

- the Quality Manual and procedures
- department manuals and procedures
- work instructions, including test, inspection and planning documents
- drawings and specifications.

The Standard requires that all documents that relate to the requirements be controlled, even though some of these may originate outside the organisation.

The control applies to all documents whether these are hard-copy documents or are held on electronic media.

## 7. PURCHASING

To ensure the Quality of the end product or service it is important to ensure the Quality of bought-in services and materials. This applies equally to component and equipment supplies and to sub-contractors. The buying company is responsible for ensuring the Quality of bought-in supplies:

- is the supplier capable of meeting the customer's requirements? This may be established by supplier assessment, verification of third-party approvals, or a review of past performance

- ensure the supplier is provided with sufficient written data to enable a complete understanding of the requirement

- ensure that products and services can only be purchased from approved suppliers

- monitor each supplier's performance and ensure corrective actions are taken where appropriate.

## 8. PRODUCT SUPPLIED BY CUSTOMERS

Items may sometimes be supplied by a customer to be built into the end product. The company should introduce a procedure to ensure these items are checked, identified, securely stored and used as specified in the contract. Similarly, customer's property (including components, equipment, documents, information) is often given into the care of the company's employees during support and service activities whether carried out on the customer's or supplier's premises. The organisation must ensure these items are adequately handled to prevent loss, damage or disclosure.

## 9. PRODUCT IDENTIFICATION AND TRACEABILITY

Procedures should enable companies to identify services, information, documents, products, sub-products, components and raw materials through the entire range of business processes. This helps prevent the possibility of items being mixed up and perhaps used incorrectly. Unique part numbers and revision numbers are a common means of achieving this objective.

Some industries may require more rigorous procedures. Defence, aerospace and medical companies may need to be able to trace every component back to its original manufacturing batch so failures can be investigated, or to enable other critical users to be traced so actions can be taken to prevent further failures. A system to ensure full traceability can be very costly and time consuming to implement. As a result, it is not a mandatory part of the Standard. Traceability should generally be specified in individual contracts unless it is an industry norm.

# 10. PROCESS CONTROL

A system should be implemented prior to commencing production to ensure process controls are adequate to ensure products and services conform to specification. The system should ensure that:

(i) the activities and equipment required to produce the product or service are identified;

(ii) instructions are prepared describing how activities are to be performed. These instructions should include details of:

- training and skills required
- set-up/start-up procedures
- the order in which activities should be carried out
- material and equipment requirements
- how the process is to be monitored
- maintenance requirements.

(iii) instructions describe how the output from a process is assessed to ensure it conforms to requirement. This can include tests, inspection methods and workmanship standards.

163

The Standard requires that essential maintenance is both provisioned and controlled. This requirement applies to any equipment which can affect the quality of the product or service supplied. It applies equally to support equipment as to equipment used in the actual production processes. For many organisations this requires the planned maintenance of computer equipment to prevent failure and down-time; it is not adaquate merely to 'fix on fail'.

'Special processes' such as heat treatment, non-destructive testing and welding are employed in some industries. The output from these processes cannot be fully assessed by subsequent inspection or testing. Deficiencies may only show up after the product is in use. These processes may well be critical in the manufacture of products such as, for example, pressure vessels. In order to ensure product quality in these circumstances it is necessary to apply additional special control procedures *during manufacturing*. These procedures govern the qualification of operators; the adequacy of operating procedures; and the continuous monitoring of conformance to procedures.

## 11. INSPECTION AND TESTING

Inspection and testing are means of assessing whether or not processes have been carried out correctly and the product conforms to specification. Inspection and testing should be considered at all stages in the production process, and be carried out where necessary. Records should be kept as evidence of the tests performed.

The Standard focuses on three principal areas in relation to test and inspection:

- receiving inspection and testing
- in process inspection and test
- final inspection and testing.

### Receiving inspection and testing

Incoming goods may be checked to ensure they conform to requirements. The type and level of inspection depends on the controls exercised by the supplier and his previous performance.

### In-process inspection and testing

In-process test and inspection procedures may be used to identify non-conforming products. Activities which monitor process parameters and indicate a likelihood of non-conforming products are generally more cost effective than inspection or test activities that only detect non-conforming products after production.

### Final inspection and testing

The appropriate level of final test and inspection may vary in the light of the overall control environment and should include a check to ensure that all the specified preceding operations have been carried out.

Tests and inspections are generally carried out after an activity has been completed. As a result, they do little other than sort 'good' product from 'bad'. Companies should therefore consider carefully the level, nature and quantity of testing/inspection introduced. Where possible, effort should be directed at preventing errors occurring in the first place. Merely finding errors once they have occurred is expensive (in terms of time and material wasted) and in itself does nothing to prevent errors occurring again in the future.

Adequate controls should exist to ensure products and services conform to specification. The control environment may be modified to take account of changes in circumstances. Individual inspection or test activities may be removed provided it can be demonstrated that process controls are adequate to prevent errors occurring. To operate a cost effective QMS, procedures should be subject to periodic review to identify appropriate prevention activities (usually process controls) which could replace test/inspection procedures.

## 12. CONTROL OF INSPECTION, MEASURING AND TEST EQUIPMENT

The performance of measuring and test equipment, including test software, is vital to product integrity for all companies which rely on test and inspection procedures to verify product conformance.

Methods and equipment used to verify that a product conforms to requirements must be reliable, used correctly and capable of performing the measurements required if credence is to be given to the results produced. The QMS should ensure that:

(i)  appropriate equipment is selected for the measurement required;

(ii)  equipment used to assure product quality is regularly calibrated to ensure readings are reliable and accurate. The calibration status should be obvious to the user;

(iii)  the calibration methods are documented to ensure traceability of the calibration to national standards. Recalibration should be performed sufficiently frequently that it occurs before equipment goes out of calibration;

(iv)  a system is in place to assess the validity of any measurement taken using an instrument which is subsequently found to be out of calibration; and

(v)  calibration records are kept for each item of measuring equipment.

## 13. INSPECTION AND TEST STATUS

It is important that products and services are labelled clearly and unambiguously to ensure anyone who may need to use it knows the inspection/test status of the item. This ensures that only proven, conforming products pass to the next stage in the process. Methods such as tags, stamps, labels, route cards, colour coding and location may be used to indicate the three test states:

- awaiting inspection/test
- passed inspection/test
- failed inspection/test.

## 14. CONTROL OF NON-CONFORMING PRODUCT

Non-conforming products and services should be clearly identified to ensure they are not used. A procedure should describe who is authorised to decide the means of disposal for non-conforming material (rework, repair, use in another application or scrap); how the decision is communicated; and how subsequent operations are controlled.

## 15. CORRECTIVE AND PREVENTIVE ACTION

A key element of any QMS is the continuous improvement of Quality. The system should ensure that actions are introduced to prevent problems from recurring. The effectiveness of the prevention activities should be verified, and any change in procedures should be properly documented and implemented. A procedure should define the responsibility for initiating and implementing corrective actions. Where possible the system should allow anyone who discovers a problem or error to highlight the need for corrective action. Specific areas where procedures are required include investigating the causes of non-conforming products and introducing actions to prevent recurrence and analysing processes, concessions, Quality records, service records and customer complaints to detect trends and introduce actions to prevent non-conforming products or services. The Standard requires documented procedures to define the actions necessary to achieve both preventive and corrective actions.

## 16. HANDLING, STORAGE, PACKAGING, PRESERVATION AND DELIVERY

A procedure is required to ensure the product is adequately packed, handled, preserved and stored to prevent damage or deterioration at all stages from the receipt of goods to safe delivery to the customer. Protection measures might include site security to prevent vandalism or theft; packing or handling procedures to protect the finish on a product; refrigeration to prevent deterioration of food; or special handling techniques to prevent, for example, damage to electronic components through electrostatic discharge.

## 17. CONTROL OF QUALITY RECORDS

Records may represent the only evidence that designated quality procedures have been applied to any given product or service. It is important to decide the nature of the records required to demonstrate this compliance, and the procedures to ensure they are properly maintained and stored. These procedures should describe:

(i)     the records required to demonstrate compliance with the requirements of the Standard;

(ii)    record storage and retrieval procedures; and

(iii)   the period for which records should be retained.

The procedures adopted should cover both hard-copy documents and electronic records, if applicable.

## 18. INTERNAL QUALITY AUDITS

To ensure the QMS is properly implemented and continues to meet the requirements of ISO 9001, procedures should be defined covering two key activities:

167

(i)     management review to ensure the QMS continues to meet the requirements of the Standard, the business and its customers. It is pointless ensuring that everyone is working to the QMS if the QMS itself is not adequate to fulfil the requirements laid down by the Standard and the business; and

(ii)    Quality audits to ensure everyone is working in accordance with the QMS. The quality audit procedure should define the following points:

- audit methods
- responsibility for scheduling and carrying out audits
- how the audit schedule will be determined
- how audit results will be recorded
- corrective action and follow-up procedures.

Auditing is a key requirement of the Standard because it is only through auditing that a company can determine whether or not the QMS is being properly implemented. It is a skilled process which should be carried out by trained personnel if it is to yield positive, beneficial results.

## 19. TRAINING

Individuals should have access to the correct procedures, tools and skills in order to carry out tasks in accordance with requirements. The appropriate skills may be acquired through a combination of qualification, training and experience. A system should be designed to identify the training needs for any activity affecting product or service quality. Detailed records should be maintained of an individual's capability to carry out specific assignments.

## 20. SERVICING

Where after-sales support is a customer requirement, for example, the regular servicing of heating equipment, provision of a tele-support helpline, or the installation of a computer network, the above procedures should be applied to the service activity to ensure it conforms to requirements.

168

## 21. STATISTICAL TECHNIQUES

Statistical techniques may sometimes be applied during the design or production of a product or service. Where these techniques are used they should be thoroughly understood and documented and based, whenever possible, on recognised techniques. Statistical techniques may include inspection sampling plans (governed by BS6001) where the acceptability of a batch of products is determined by the inspection of a sample, statistical process control where the control of a process is determined by monitoring the control parameters and statistical sampling and analysis to select a representative sample and then to analyse the results when carrying out research, or market surveys.

# Appendix 2

## QUALITY POLICY MANUAL

OMEGA UK Ltd
75 Gamma Street
Ilkley
West Yorkshire

This document defines the Quality Policy of Omega UK Ltd. It has been compiled to meet the requirements of ISO9001 1994 and similar national and international standards. The document is Company Confidential. All procedures contained herein are mandatory within the company. This policy manual is to be read in conjunction with the operating procedures of the company which have been prepared and issued to meet the needs of the company and the requirements for quality system certification.

169

Compiled:     J. Gray

Approved:     S. Baldwin

Date of Issue:     March 1995

COPY NUMBER: SEVEN

NOTE

Numbered copies of this document have been issued to registered holders. These copies will be maintained. Amendments to unnumbered copies will not be issued.

**OMEGA UK LIMITED**

ISSUE CONTROL

The Quality Director of Omega UK Limited is responsible for authorising changes to this document.

The reference number and issue number of the Quality Manual is identified on the front page and each subsequent page of the document.

Alterations will result in a change to the issue status and complete reissue of the overall document.

Records of all changes to ther Quality Manual will be maintained by the Quality Director for audit purposes and a summary will be provided within the Quality Manual itself.

Record of Changes

| Issue No | Date issued | Summary of Change |
|---|---|---|
| 1 | April 1992 | New Manual |
| 2 | March 1993 | Management review added |
| 3 | March 1995 | Total review to ensure compliance with 1994 Standard |

## CONTENTS

171

**OMEGA UK LIMITED**

QM001
ISSUE 3
Page 4 of 17

SCOPE OF THE ORGANISATION

OMEGA UK LIMITED is responsible for marketing, selling, distributing, and providing customer support and training services for the complete range of Instrumentation Control products throughout the UK. Omega UK also acts as a focus to ensure UK requirements are fed into future product development activities throughout The Alpha Group. Omega UK is based in Ilkley, North Yorks, and employs approximately 200 staff.

The UK sales and distribution activities are supported by two key groups:

(i)   The customer support unit provides technical advice and product support to customers and internal commercial functions.

(ii)  The training group provides training to employees and to customers. The training consists of both standard packages and bespoke courses designed to fulfil a specific customer requirement.

This document defines the procedures and controls which have been implemented to ensure products and services are produced under controlled conditions so they conform to customer requirements.

The Company is introducing a 'Total Quality' approach as a basis for its operations. This will complement its existing Quality Management system and make every individual responsible for the quality of their contribution. Every supervisor and manager has a responsibility for ensuring this policy is understood and followed at all times.

DESIGN CONTROL

Product design is not carried out by Omega UK Ltd. Product design and manufacture is carried out by Omega International in the UK, who are suppliers to Omega UK Ltd.

However, Omega UK has an important part in the design process. It can provide data to use as a basis for ensuring customer needs are met. Senior staff of Omega UK attend periodic design reviews to monitor the progress of new product designs. Records of these design reviews are maintained by the design authorities.

Omega UK Ltd is responsible for designing the training courses delivered by its employees. The system to address the design control requirement for the training group is covered in paragraph 4 of this manual.

**OMEGA UK LIMITED**  QM001
ISSUE 3
Page 5 of 17

QUALITY POLICY

We, the management and employees of Omega UK Ltd, are committed to providing our customers with the products and services they want, at a profit to us. To achieve this we require everyone to strive constantly to improve the quality of the products and services we supply.

To that end OMEGA UK has developed an organisation which is geared to respond promptly and effectively to every client enquiry. Key to this organisation is the Quality Management System based on ISO9001 which I and the management team believe is critical to the successful implementation of this policy.

173

S. Baldwin

S.Baldwin
General Manager

---

**OMEGA UK LIMITED**                                    QM001
                                                        ISSUE 3
                                                        Page 6 of 17

---

1.  INTRODUCTION

1.1  Applicability

This document shall apply to all work undertaken by the company unless covered in Quality Plans detailing specific contract requirements. It forms the company's response to the requirements of ISO9001.

1.2  Applicable documents

(i)    ISO9001

(ii)   Company Quality Manual (this document)

(iii)  Departmental operating procedures and instructions

(iv)   Project Quality Plans – as appropriate.

1.3  General

Procedures and activities detailed within this document are designed to ensure that the product or service supplied to the customer satisfies all contractual requirements.

This document is intended to cover all aspects of the work undertaken within the defined 'scope' of the organisation, and in so doing, to satisfy the requirements of ISO9001.

In the event of conflict between this document and specific contractual requirements, then the latter shall take precedence.

2.  ORGANISATION (ISO9001 para.4.1)

The Management organisation for Quality is structured around a QA Group under a full-time Quality Director.

The Quality Director is responsible to the General Manager for the resolution of all matters pertaining to Quality. He also has a functional responsibility to the Alpha Group Quality Director who is responsible for Corporate Quality worldwide.

The General Manager is responsible for the management of Omega UK Limited. All department heads report directly to him. The Quality

Director has the authority and seniority necessary to carry out his responsibilities and ensure the integrity of the Quality Management System.

Each manager is responsible for ensuring that customer satisfaction is achieved within the area for which he is responsible. The achievement of Quality objectives will have a priority at least equal to his other business objectives. Formal customer complaints are dealt with by the appropriate manager and are monitored directly by the General Manager.

The management structure at Omega UK Ltd changes as company objectives evolve. Detailed organisational charts are not included in this document: charts of the current structure can be provided on request and are available to each employee for reference.

3.    CONTRACT REVIEW (ISO9001 para.4.3)

REFERENCES

(i)   QP05   Contract Review
(ii)   DP6.1   Order Entry

Planning is conducted as follows:

3.1    Customer Enquiries

On receipt of a customer enquiry a review is conducted to ensure all aspects of the customer's enquiry can be met. In order to determine this, a degree of planning will take place which will result in the production of a formal proposal.

3.2    Contracts

All incoming orders and contracts are reviewed before acceptance. On receipt of a contract, a review is conducted to ensure it reflects the conditions agreed at the proposal stage, or that variations are agreed and accepted by the Company once the full implications are known and understood.

Particular attention is paid to requirements that are considered to be special or unusual by reason of newness, unfamiliarity or absence of precedents. Contracts containing specific requirements relating to product performance, quality or customer surveillance must be approved by the Quality Director before acceptance.

4.　DESIGN CONTROL (ISO9001 para.4.4)

REFERENCES

(i)　DP13.1 Training course design and verification

(ii)　DP13.2 Course documentation

(iii)　DP13.3 Course administration

(iv)　DP13.4 Course feedback and improvement

Omega UK Ltd undertakes the design and delivery of courses for internal and external customers. Standard courses may be developed to meet an identified general customer requirement, or a course may be designed specifically for a customer. Internal courses may be product related or general management skills training. The need for new internal courses is generally identified by means of a regular training needs analysis, or as a result of the annual appraisal system.

External customer needs are identified either by the marketing department or by the sales force. Any specific external customer requirement is subject to the normal contract review process.

Once a requirement for a course has been established, course design takes place following the control procedures listed above. The purpose of these procedures is to ensure the following:

a)　Clear input requirements are agreed before the design process begins. These may be agreed by external or internal customers.

b)　The design process itself is approached in a logical, structured way and is carried out by trained, skilled personnel.

c)　The design output follows a standard format which ensures consistent course delivery.

d)　The design group verify that the design meets the input requirements before the course is launched.

e)　When courses are being delivered, customer satisfaction is monitored and used as a basis for making improvements.

176

5.   QUALITY SYSTEM DOCUMENT CONTROL and
     RECORDS (ISO9001 para. 4.2; 4.5; 4.16)

REFERENCES

(i)  QP01  Control of Procedures

5.1   Quality system documentation

OMEGA UK has established a documented quality management
system based on the requirements of ISO9001 and covering the entire
activities of the UK organisation. The documentation set comprises:

  (a)  Quality Policy Manual (this document)
  (b)  Operating Procedures which define the requirements and
       objectives of each operating process of the organisation
  (c)  Local Work Instructions for specific tasks where the absence of
       such instructions could be prejudicial to the correct
       performance of the process.

The need for specific new procedures to meet the requirements of a
contract, or the needs of the business will be identified during the
Contract Review Stage or as a result of the Quality System audit and
review process.

All working procedures and instructions are controlled documents,
subject to authorisation and issue control. QP01 defines the system
used to ensure control is effective, and that only authorised documents
are available for use. Documents are authorised or approved by the
process owner for technical content and on behalf of the general
manager as evidence of management commitment to each process
definition.

5.2   Work Instructions

Due to the nature of the work undertaken by the company and the skill
level and experience of employees, work instructions will not normally
be necessary in order to meet general contract requirements.

5.3   Records

Records are maintained of:

  (a) Corrective actions following an identified failure
  (b) Customer complaints and actions taken
  (c) Management review
  (d) System audits and supplier audits

**OMEGA UK LIMITED**                                    QM001
                                                         ISSUE 3
                                                      Page 10 of 17

(e) Any inspection activity performed

(f) Contract reviews

(g) Customer satisfaction surveys and actions taken

(h) Design planning and verification activities

The requirement to keep records and a definition of the records to be kept is defined within the procedures. Records are maintained by archiving and by conformance to the relevant documentation and control procedures. Records are retained for two years unless a contract requires a different period.

6.    PURCHASING (ISO9001 para.4.6)

REFERENCES

(i)    DP6.2  Supplier control

(ii)   DP6.3  Purchasing

(iii)  DP7.1  Product receipt

The above procedures detail the controls used to ensure purchased goods and services are fit for their intended purpose and are obtained only from capable sources.

6.1    Receiving Inspection (ISO9001 para.4.10)

The general policy is not to carry out inspection of product received from sister companies within the Alpha Group unless this is required for specific contracts when it will be specified within the quality plan for the contract.

All externally procured items will be subject to inspection/validation procedures, commensurate with the risks involved in using the item, before being put to use.

7.    CUSTOMER SUPPLIED PRODUCT (ISO9001 para.4.7)

REFERENCES

(i)    QP05  Contract review

(ii)   DP7.1  Product receipt

(iii)  DP7.2  Warehousing and distribution

178

**OMEGA UK LIMITED**                    QM001
                                        ISSUE 3
                                        Page 11 of 17

---

All material and information supplied by the customer for the purpose of fulfilling contract requirements will be maintained in accordance with the requirements of that customer. The need for specific procedures for the control and maintenance of customer supplied material will be identified during contract appraisal.

8.  IDENTIFICATION and INDICATION OF INSPECTION STATUS (ISO9001 para.4.8 and 4.12)

REFERENCES

(i)    DP7.2  Warehousing and distribution

(ii)   DP7.3  Product audit

(iii)  DP13.1  Course design and verification

OMEGA product and the documentation systems that support both the client and the product are discretely identified to facilitate the identification of similar but differing product and documentation. OMEGA UK procedures define the documentation identification system.

No product manufacture is undertaken by Omega UK Ltd. Product identification is initiated and maintained throughout the manufacturing process. All product is received by Omega with a unique serial number indicating type, date and batch of manufacture. This identification is maintained throughout the storage and distribution process.

Where product inspection is carried out, the use of controlled inspection stamps and stock locations determines the 'inspection status' of the product in accordance with the prescribed operating procedures.

All courses designed by Omega UK Ltd are stamped 'DRAFT' and dated, until approval has been given for release. Once verified and released for delivery, each course is dated using a standard format in a page 'header'. This ensures that a course cannot be made available until it has passed the verification process.

9.   PROCESS CONTROL (ISO9001 para.4.9)

REFERENCES

(i)   QP01  Control of procedures

(ii)  DP7.3  Product modifications

(iii) DP7.2  Warehousing and distribution

(iv)  Support Manual

(v)   Administration Manual

(vi)  DP13.3  Course administration

Omega UK Ltd is primarily an administration, logistics and support activity. Procedures are developed in accordance with QP01 for all activities. These define how each process operates and is controlled, the inputs and outputs required and how conformance to the requirements is demonstrated. Omega UK Ltd has a policy of understanding and controlling processes so errors can be prevented, rather than detecting and reworking errors after the event. All procedures are subject to the document control procedures outlined in paragraph 5.

10.   IN-PROCESS AND FINAL INSPECTION AND TESTING (ISO9001 para.4.10)

REFERENCES

(i)  DP7.3  Product audit

The general policy is not to carry out inspection of product received from sister companies within the Alpha Group where a high degree of confidence exists in the product.

If release inspection is required in a specific contract, this will be identified during the contract review and included in the contract quality plan. Procedure DP7.3 describes how this activity is planned and carried out if required in a specific contract or if evidence indicates it is necessary.

Release documentation is prepared as required by contract using established records as evidence for release decisions. This documentation defines the 'product' delivered and certifies compliance with contractual requirements.

11.  CONTROL OF INSPECTION, MEASURING AND TEST
     EQUIPMENT (ISO9001 para.4.11)

REFERENCES

(i)  QP03  Calibration

(ii) DP10.1  MIS procedures

Due to the nature of the work undertaken by Omega UK Ltd,
equipment of this nature will rarely be required.

Where a specific requirement exists it is the responsibility of the person
using such equipment to ensure that it is calibrated before use. This
will be traceable to National Standards and will be carried out in
accordance with QP03. All calibrations will be certified. Calibrated
equipment will bear as a minimum a printed label indicating the period
of validity of the equipment's calibration.

This printed label will conform with established practice, either for the
site on which the work is performed or that from which the equipment
was obtained (e.g. an equipment hire company). In this way the
authenticity of calibration can be verified at any time.

Product used to support internal processes (particularly MIS) is
subject to regular assessment and service by specialist contractors.
This process is described in the MIS procedures.

12.  CONTROL OF NON-CONFORMING PRODUCT (ISO9001
     para.4.13)

REFERENCES

(i)   DP7.1  Product receipt

(ii)  DP7.2  Warehousing and distribution

(iii) DP7.3  Product audit

(iv)  DP12.1  Customer returns

(v)   Course design and verification

Non-conforming material will be suitably identified and segregated to
prevent its inadvertent use. Investigation into the reason for non-
conformance will take place and the necessary corrective action
implemented.

181

**OMEGA UK LIMITED**  QM001
ISSUE 3
Page 14 of 17

13.  CORRECTIVE and PREVENTIVE ACTION (ISO9001 para.4.14)

REFERENCES

(i)  QP04  Reporting results and corrective action

(ii)  DP13.4  Course feedback and improvement

(iii)  QP02  System audit and management review

Corrective and preventive action is an essential element in an effective and constantly improving Quality System. OMEGA UK has documented systems for dealing with both product and system deficiencies. All customer complaints are referred to the highest level of the organisation and are also subject to a general review as part of the management review process. Effective corrective actions require:

- good reporting systems
- analysis of reports
- implementation of the immediate solution to correct the problem
- instigation of longer-term action to investigate the root cause of the problem and introduce preventive measures to prevent recurrence.

13.1  Reporting

Defect reports, covering both product and system problems, will be recorded and will result in an investigation into the defect and instigation of the necessary corrective action.

13.2  Analysis, corrective and preventive action

Defects are analysed. Problem areas, or potential problem areas, are notified to appropriate managers and, if necessary, subcontractors who will take the necessary corrective action in order to prevent recurrence.

Records will be maintained of the actions taken.

## 14. HANDLING, STORAGE, PACKAGING, PRESERVATION AND DELIVERY (ISO9001 para 4.15)

REFERENCES

(i) DP7.1 Product receipt
(ii) DP7.3 Warehousing and distribution
(iii) DP7.3 Product audit
(iv) DP13.3 Course administration

Product is received from the supplier in packaging suitable for onward shipment. Delivery is made by an established courier using approved packaging, marking, shipment and control methods. Good commercial practice will be applied to the safe handling, storage and delivery of hardware, software, and supporting documentation. This will be controlled in accordance with contract requirements and specific procedures identified as necessary during contract review. There are no particular requirements associated with product preservation. Performance indices are generated for the product handling and despatch function to monitor service failures experienced by clients or the company.

Delivery of training seminars is monitored by means of client surveys carried out at the conclusion of each course.

## 15. QUALITY AUDIT AND MANAGEMENT REVIEW (ISO9001 para.4.1; 4.17)

REFERENCES

(i) QP02 System audit and management review
(ii) Departmental procedures

Audits of the Quality System are performed across the organisation in accordance with a planned audit schedule. The objective of the audit is twofold:

a) To ensure procedures exist and are adequate to ensure compliance with the appropriate standards.
b) To ensure procedures have been complied with. Personal awareness of the procedural requirements provides evidence that procedures are currently being applied. Certified records of work done and results achieved provide evidence that procedures have been applied in the past.

**OMEGA UK LIMITED**

QM001
ISSUE 3
Page 16 of 17

Prior to preparing the audit schedule, and as a part of each audit, the Quality System documentation will be reviewed to determine compatibility with the objectives of the business and continued compliance with Quality Standards. Audits are conducted only by staff trained in the skills of auditing and are supervised by the Quality Director.

Management reviews of the Quality Systems are conducted annually by the senior management of the organisation to ensure they meet the perceived needs of the business and the requirements of the appropriate Quality Management System approvals in accordance with the recommendations of ISO9001 para.4.1.5.

This review will address the findings of previous audits, reported customer problems and the effectiveness of corrective actions.

16.   TRAINING (ISO9001 para.4.18)

REFERENCES

(i)    DP13.5  Performance appraisal
(ii)   DP13.6  Training records
(iii)  DP13.7  Training needs analysis

The company considers training to be essential to the continued success of the business. Training needs are identified within the organisation in one of two ways:

a)  The annual appraisal of each individual by their immediate supervisor is designed to identify training required to enable them to carry out their job.
b)  The annual analysis of training needs identifies company-wide training needs which the training department is required to meet.

All training needs of the organisation are met wherever possible by the training group. Where this is not possible, the training group will recommend an external course to fulfil the need.

The annual business planning activity ensures all identified training needs have been reviewed and adequate financial provision made to meet the requirements. The training group maintains training records for each individual. These detail the identified training needs and record how the need was met.

184

17.   SERVICING (ISO9001 para.4.19)

REFERENCES

(i)   DP13.1  Course design and verification

(ii)  Support manual

The need to support training courses once they have been delivered is considered during the design of new courses. This includes the provision where required for a follow-up session to discuss problems encountered by the attendees in using the skills learned. It also embraces the need to ensure skilled trainers are available to deliver the course for a minimum of two years after initial launch.

Product design is not undertaken by Omega UK Ltd. The UK customer support group does, however, have an input into the design process to ensure support issues are catered for. The Quality Systems of Omega Design Ltd define the after-sales support requirements which must be met before a product can be launched worldwide. The product will not be accepted for sale into the UK unless these requirements have been met.

185

18.   STATISTICAL TECHNIQUES (ISO9001 para.4.20)

REFERENCES

(i)   DP7.3  Product audit

As part of the distribution activity a degree of sample inspection and testing may be performed. This is carried out in accordance with BS6001. No statistical process control is carried out by the company.

# Appendix 3

**OMEGA UK LIMITED**

Document Number QP01
Revision Level: 2
Page 1 of 6

## DOCUMENT CONTROL

This procedure is issued and controlled by the Quality department. Changes may only be authorised by the General Manager, together with the Quality Director. This is a controlled document subject to automatic update and so should not be copied.

ONLY SIGNED AUTHORISED COPIES MAY BE USED AS WORKING DOCUMENTS.

Originator .....*J Smith*..................... Date *1st March 1995*...........

Authorised:

Quality Director ......*J. Gray*............... Date *1st March 1995*..........

General Manager .....*S. Baldwin*......... Date *1st March 1995*..........

Date of issue: March 1995

| OMEGA UK LIMITED | Document Number: QP01 |
|---|---|
| | Revision Level: 2 |
| | Page 2 of 6 |

DOCUMENT REVISION POLICY

The Quality Director of Omega UK Limited is responsible for authorising changes to this document.

The reference number and revision status of this document are identified on the front page and each subsequent page of the document.

Any alterations will result in a change to the revision status and complete reissue of the total document.

Records of all changes made to the procedures will be maintained by the Quality Director and a summary will be provided within the document itself.

Record of Changes

| Revision | Date issued | Summary of Change |
|---|---|---|
| 1 | August 1992 | Initial issue |
| 2 | March 1995 | Relaxation of format requirements and addition of section on control of non-Omega documents |

**OMEGA UK LIMITED**  Document Number QP01
Revision Level: 2
Page 3 of 6

## 1.0   Purpose and Scope

Procedures describe the way we carry out and control all the operations which affect the quality of our products and services. It is essential that procedures are documented, easy to use, cover all the required areas and are controlled so everyone is working to the same version of any procedure. This procedure covers two areas:

a)  The standard format of a procedure document.

b)  The controls required to ensure only the authorised, latest version of procedure documents are available for use.

## 2.0   Responsibility

The manager of each department is responsible for the issue and control of procedures which ensure this procedure is followed. The Quality Director is responsible for ensuring that the system for controlling the issue of procedures meets the requirements of ISO9001.

## 3.0   References

ISO9001 para 4.5

## 4.0   Definitions: Controlled document

Controlled documents are subject to a system to ensure everyone using the document is working to the same version of that document. Controlled documents are documents considered to define activities and processes whose operation is critical to the success and efficient operation of the company. Within such documents requirements are stated and methods described which can only be changed by management agreement. By requiring everyone to operate in accordance with the defined requirements, and controlling the document change process, the process definition is controlled and can only be changed with the formal knowledge and agreement of all interested parties.

**OMEGA UK LIMITED**                    Document Number QP01
Revision Level: 2
Page 4 of 6

---

### 5.0   Procedures

### 5.1   Format of Procedures

All procedures issued by Omega UK Ltd will follow the format specified in this procedure. While this is the preferred format, particular circumstances may require deviation from this layout. Details of the preferred format are as follows:

5.1.1   The front page will carry the following information:

Document number and revision
Page 1 of y (y = no. of pages in document)
Title of procedure
Name of originator
Signature of person authorising procedure
Date of issue
A statement on control of the procedure as follows:

'This procedure is issued and controlled by the . . . . . . . department. Changes may only be authorised by the . . . . . . Manager. This is a controlled document subject to automatic update and so should not be copied.

ONLY SIGNED AUTHORISED COPIES MAY BE USED AS WORKING DOCUMENTS.'

The person(s) required to authorise any procedure will be agreed by the department manager and the Quality Director.

5.1.2   All subsequent pages will carry the following information:

Document number and revision
Page x of y.

5.1.3   The format of the text will generally be as follows:

**1.0   Purpose and scope**

Reason the procedure is required and the activities to which it applies.

**2.0 Responsibilities**

The people responsible (by job title) for ensuring the procedure is followed.

**3.0 References**

Documents referred to in the procedure (e.g. other procedures, National Standards, manual, etc.).

**4.0 Definitions**

An explanation of abbreviations and any non-standard terms used in the text.

**5.0 Procedure**

Main body of the procedure explaining what is done and how it is done. This should be sufficiently detailed to ensure the essentials of the process are documented and controlled, but not so detailed that every minor change in the process requires the procedure to be amended.

5.1.4 Appendices may be included to show standard forms etc. used in the process. Page 2 of the document will always be the revision record sheet for that document.

**5.2 Control of Procedures**

5.2.1 All masters are kept within the department responsible for their issue and control. They may be kept as hard copies or on a computer system. Access to the procedures to make changes must be restricted to the person(s) authorised on page 1 of the procedure.

5.2.2 Each department must establish and maintain a master list showing the latest status and distribution record for all their documents. The department must ensure recipients sign for any updates. The person issuing the procedure is responsible for ensuring the old procedure is returned and destroyed; this ensures that only the current version is in use at any time.

**OMEGA UK LIMITED**                    Document Number QP01
                                              Revision Level: 2
                                                Page 6 of 6

5.2.3   If procedures are issued via a computer system, rather than as hard copies, then a system must ensure they cannot be printed off or, if they are printed, then the words 'UNCONTROLLED COPY' appear on the front page.

5.2.4   The Quality Manager will maintain a copy of all obsolete documents so the nature of any change to a procedure can be identified, if required.

**5.3     Revision Status**

5.3.1   The identification of each document will be through a combined generic number and a suffix – the revision status. The reference number is individual to the document and may be supplemented by a title for general use; document numbers are allocated by the Quality Director.

5.3.2.  The revision number identifies the difference between copies of what could appear to be identical documents. The revision status for all approved documents will be numeric and will increase by one for each new version of the document.

Thus document QP01 revision 2 is a later version of a similar document QP01 revision 1.

5.3.3   The second page of each procedural document will contain a history of the revisions to that document in a format similar to that shown on page 2 of this document.

**5.4     Control of non-company documents**

5.4.1   Control of documents which originate outside Omega UK Ltd may also be crucial in controlling the products and services which we supply. Control of these documents will require separate arrangements; these will be agreed on a case-by-case basis between the manager concerned with their use and the Quality Director.

# Appendix 4

## QUALITY SYSTEM AUDIT and MANAGEMENT REVIEW

This procedure is issued and controlled by the Quality Department. Changes may only be authorised by the General Manager together with the Quality Director. This is a controlled document subject to automatic update and so should not be copied.

193

ONLY SIGNED AUTHORISED COPIES MAY BE USED AS WORKING DOCUMENTS

Originator ..... *J Smith* ..... Date ..... 1st March 1995

Authorised:

Quality Director ..... *J. Gray* ..... Date ..... 1st March 1995

General Manager ..... *S. Baldwin* ..... Date ..... 1st March 1995

Date of issue: March 1995

**OMEGA UK LIMITED**

Document Number: QP02
Revision Level: 2
Page 2 of 8

DOCUMENT REVISION POLICY

The Quality Director of Omega UK Limited is responsible for authorising changes to this document.

The reference number and revision status of this document are identified on the front page and each subsequent page of the document.

Any alterations will result in a change to the revision status and complete reissue of the total document.

194

Records of all changes made to the procedures will be maintained by the Quality Director and a summary will be provided within the document itself.

Record of Changes

| Revision | Date issued | Summary of Change |
|---|---|---|
| 1 | May 1993 | Initial issue |
| 2 | March 1995 | General changes to section 5 of the procedure and addition of section 6 |

## 1.0 Purpose and Scope

The purpose of system audit and review is to provide management information on the operation of the Quality Management System (QMS). This enables management to ensure the Quality Management System meets the needs of the business and the requirements of the Quality System Standards. Audit and review have the following objectives:

Quality System Audit:

(i) To ensure the documented Quality System meets the requirements of the Quality System Standard (ISO9001).
(ii) To ensure the documented system is practical, understood and followed throughout the business.

Management Review:

(i) A regular management review of the QMS to ensure it is effective in meeting the needs of the business and assuring product and service quality whilst meeting the requirements of ISO9001. This is achieved by identifying and monitoring key quality performance parameters.

## 2.0 Responsibilities

It is the responsibility of the Quality Director to ensure this procedure is followed throughout the organisation. Functional heads will have prior knowledge of the audit programme and will ensure that staff are available to support its demands.

## 3.0 References

ISO9001 sections 4.1 and 4.17.

## 4.0 Definitions

QMS Quality Management System

**OMEGA UK LIMITED**                    Document Number: QP02
                                        Revision Level: 2
                                        Page 4 of 8

---

**5.0   Procedures**

**5.1   Quality System Audit**

**5.1.1   Audit Schedule**

Quality System audits will be carried out in accordance with an audit schedule produced annually by the Quality Director. The schedule will be based on known problem areas and the results of previous audits.

The audit schedule will define the area of the business and the QMS feature to be audited. Over time, all areas of the business and each requirement of the Standard will be audited. This pre-planned audit schedule will be subject to change to reflect the perceived needs of the business, particularly where evidence of system deficiency indicates a need for additional audits which may not have been planned at the start of the cycle. Provision will be made within the audit schedule for showing the status of each audit and for the addition of audits not previously planned.

**5.1.2   Audit Planning**

To be effective it is essential that audits are planned, executed and reported in a systematic manner. After allocating an auditor to fulfil an audit requirement, management will allow adequate time for the auditor to plan his programme of work.

In planning the audit, the auditor will first seek to understand the requirements of the ISO Standard, and the way in which the company has chosen to fulfil the requirements of the Standard. This will involve a review of all the documentation pertaining to the operation of the area being audited, including a review of previous audit results and corrective actions implemented.

The output of the planning activity will be a plan of how the audit is to be carried out. This plan may include checklists to guide the questioning and ensure that the audit is structured. This list must not, however, be a total list of questions to be ticked off as they are asked. Auditing is a process of investigation with no pre-determined conclusion. Questioning should be structured and reactive to the answers received. A checklist should ensure that major issues are dealt with in an ordered way during the audit, but will require auditor understanding to adapt as the audit proceeds.

**OMEGA UK LIMITED**

Document Number: QP02
Revision Level: 2
Page 5 of 8

### 5.1.3   Audit Execution

All audits will be carried out by qualified and experienced auditors independent of the department being audited. Generally the auditors will be accredited assessors registered under the National Scheme for Assessors of Quality Management Systems.

The purpose of the audit is to gather information to demonstrate that the QMS is:

(i)   adequate to meet the requirement of the Quality System Standard; and

(ii)  understood and followed in the area being audited.

For a QMS to be effective it must reflect the requirements of the Standard and be understood and followed by the user. The auditor should gather 'objective evidence' of conformance to the requirement. During the audit, the user must demonstrate to the auditor an understanding of the QMS. Personal awareness of the procedural requirements provides evidence that procedures are currently being applied. Certified records of work done and results achieved provide evidence that procedures have been applied in the past.

Auditors should use open-ended questions so that the auditee must make a committed answer and not simply a positive or negative response. Auditors should conduct a line of questioning to reach a conclusion and must gather sufficient evidence to support that conclusion: auditor training provides training on the degree of evidence required. Where tangible evidence is obtained, this should be referenced in the audit report.

### 5.1.4   Audit Reporting

The output of the audit will be an audit report. This report will be identified by a unique reference derived form the audit plan and will contain, as a minimum:

(i)   a statement of the audit investigation performed; the activity audited, standards, procedures, individuals and processes;

(ii)  the evidence gathered, including reference to documents etc.; and

**OMEGA UK LIMITED**

Document Number: QP02
Revision Level: 2
Page 6 of 8

(iii) any deficiencies identified. This will be recorded in sufficient detail to permit subsequent independent re-audit.

The following must be agreed and documented for any identified deficiencies:

(i) corrective actions required;
(ii) person responsible for corrective actions; and
(iii) timescale for implementation.

It is the responsibility of the auditee, together with the manager of the audited area, to determine the actions required to correct the audit deficiencies. A timescale for the corrective actions will be a standard 28 days. Exceptionally, a longer time may be accepted but the reasons for this delay will be defined in the audit report.

Each audit report should be circulated to:

- the department manager of the area audited
- the General Manager
- the Quality Director
- the audit file.

**5.1.5  Corrective action and audit follow-up**

It is the responsibility of the department manager to agree and implement the required corrective action. It is the responsibility of the auditor to follow up and re-audit the corrective actions, and record formally when the action has been satisfactorily completed and the audit closed.

Where the agreed action has not taken place and/or such action has not resulted in correction of the deficiency, the report will be updated and reissued to show the outstanding situation and copied to the original recipients of the report.

**5.2  Management Review**

**5.2.1  Planning**

A Management Review will be held annually to review the effectiveness of the QMS in meeting the needs of the business and

**OMEGA UK LIMITED**

Document Number: QP02
Revision Level: 2
Page 7 of 8

satisfying the requirements of the Standards. The meeting will be chaired by the General Manager and will involve all members of the Senior Management Team. A secretary will be nominated to record and subsequently distribute the minutes of the meeting.

Prior to the meeting the Quality Director will provide a summary report on the operation of the quality system; additional data will be presented at the meeting as each topic is discussed.

At the review meeting, functional heads will provide a summary of the activities for which they are responsible and will also outline their experiences with the operation of the Quality Management System, including any failures to comply. The meeting will also discuss the organisation's Quality Policy and either change it or re-affirm their commitment to its aims and goals.

The Quality Director will be responsible for following up any actions arising, and reporting on these at regular management meetings.

### 5.2.2 Execution

The following areas will be considered in each Management Review:

(i) customer complaints;

(ii) failure statistics, warranty and post-warranty;

(iii) post-sales enquiries; types of query and time to close;

(iv) vendor performance;

(v) Internal Quality System Audits of QMS, areas audited, deficiencies identified, corrective actions implemented and actions outstanding;

(vi) repair turnaround times;

(vii) any customer-specific performance measurements required, as described in the Quality Plan;

(viii) customer feedback results;

(ix) quality costs;

(x) the Quality Policy;

199

---

**OMEGA UK LIMITED**

Document Number: QP02
Revision Level: 2
Page 8 of 8

---

(xi)   training needs; and

(xii)  any other quality-related problems.

### 5.2.3   Corrective action

The Management Team will agree timescales and responsibilities for the implementation of recommendations and corrective actions. These will be formally recorded in the minutes. These minutes will outline the subjects discussed, the decisions reached and the actions allocated and accepted. These minutes will be circulated to the attendees and to any other individuals concerned with carrying out the resultant actions; a copy will also be retained in the central audit file.

The Quality Director will verify the implementation of the recommendations and corrective actions within the agreed timescales.

# Appendix 5

## BUSINESS PLANNING

This document defines the process and activities associated with the generation of an annual business plan, and outlines the supplementary planning processes that ensure the successful implementation of the approved plan.

Management of this document, the system it describes, and the control of changes to the procedure is vested in the General Manager. He alone has the authority to agree changes to the content of this document.

<u>201</u>

ONLY SIGNED AUTHORISED COPIES MAY BE USED AS WORKING DOCUMENTS

Originator ....*J Smith*.................... Date ...*1st March 1995*......

Authorised:

General Manager ...*S. Baldwin*........ Date ...*1st March 1995*......

Date of issue: March 1995

**OMEGA UK LIMITED**

Document Number: CGN003
Revision Level: 1
Page 2 of 7

## DOCUMENT REVISION POLICY

The General Manager of Omega UK Ltd is responsible for authorising changes to this document.

The reference number and revision status of this document are identified on the front page and each subsequent page of the document.

Any alterations will result in a change to the revision status and complete reissue of the total document.

Records of all changes made to the procedures will be maintained by the Quality Director and a summary will be provided within the document itself.

Record of Changes

| Revision | Date | Summary of Change |
|----------|------|-------------------|
| 1 | May 1995 | Initial issue |

**OMEGA UK LIMITED**

Document Number: CGN003
Revision Level: 1
Page 3 of 7

### 1.0 Purpose and Scope

The purpose of this document is to define the requirements to plan the objectives of the Omega UK Ltd business, and to have these business objectives agreed and then used to define individual and group contributions to the overall plan. The document defines the need for an annual business plan and supporting plans for the business functions, and in this respect is mandatory. It outlines the format of the Business Plan but in this respect is subsidiary to the Corporate definition of such plans which is laid down at the start of the annual business planning cycle.

### 2.0 Responsibilities

It is the responsibility of the General Manager to ensure that a business plan is produced in accordance with the requirements of corporate directives. It is the responsibility of the General Manager to ensure that agreed business objectives are achieved through the efficient use of the available resources, and defined through the production and development of local business plans which reflect the corporate requirements.

### 3.0 References

(i)   ISO9001 para. 4.3
(ii)  Procedure CGN005 – Marketing
(iii) Alpha – Business Planning Requirements
(iv)  Corporate business planning requirements from time to time
      issued by the Executive Board of Directors

### 4.0 Procedure

### 4.1 The Omega Business Plan

On receipt of a requirement to produce the annual Business Plan the General Manager will allocate specific responsibilities to local directors to provide core information, and particularly financial information, to create a baseline for a budget of costs and income for the next financial year. When the data has been gathered and assessed by those nominated by the General Manager the Business Plan will be compiled in accordance will the prescribed rules.

203

**OMEGA UK LIMITED**

Document Number: CGN003
Revision Level: 1
Page 4 of 7

Using the model provided by Alpha, this data will be analysed to produce a reasoned view of the current year's performance and a prediction of what is possible for the following year.

The Business Plan will generally follow the format shown in Appendix 1. The typical headings shown there are for guidance only and do not constitute a requirement separate from the corporate direction of this process. The content of each element of the plan will address those issues required by the corporate organisation.

Each assessment and prediction will be justified and supported wherever possible with data. All necessary expenses, capital and revenue, needed to support the business during the ensuing year will be quantified and explained, together with the assumptions on which they are based.

Changes of stategy or policy will similarly be documented, particularly if such changes are fundamental to the assessment of future business performance.

On completion of the planning process the Business Plan will be reviewed by the General Manager and such staff as he may nominate, and after adjustment will be reviewed and approved by the Alpha Board.

In the event that the corporate organisation requires changes or clarification to the plan such changes will be made and the document re-submitted for approval. Such iterations may continue but eventually the Plan will become the official and approved Business Plan for Omega UK Ltd.

It is now the responsibility of the General Manager to ensure that the overall plan is converted to individual and group plans in order that responsibilities and authorities are known and understood and the overall objectives are met.

This transfer will be done through the medium of performance plans for each of the local directors and key managers, which will then form the basis of their own action plans for the coming year.

204

## 4.2  Sales Planning

The overall objectives for the sales plan are contained within the Business Plan. It is the responsibility of the General Manager to ensure that the Sales organisation is organised and motivated to produce the results predicted in the Business Plan. He will achieve this by a combination of organisational appointments and motivational techniques.

The General Manager will establish an organisation for ensuring adequate sales cover for the product and territory, allocating resources in an appropriate manner under sales area managers. Each sales manager will be allocated a sector of business and will be required to generate sales in accordance with his personal segment of the Business Plan which will be conveyed to him in the form of a compensation plan and objectives arising from his annual appraisal. Sales staff will be allocated to nominated sales managers and they too will have objectives and compensation plans that reflect in part the requirements placed upon their local manager.

A synthesis of all compensation plans and objectives throughout the organisation should produce a reasonable representation of the company Business Plan.

## 4.3  Marketing Plans

The Marketing function will also produce a Marketing Business Plan in support of the annual planning round. The purpose of this plan is to define and control the company's expenditure on marketing through the year.

This plan, together with the operating procedures of the function establish business objectives and a methodology for achieving those objectives in a defined controlled and auditable manner. Procedure CGN005 defines the processes that lead to the development of the marketing plan.

205

OMEGA UK LIMITED

Document Number: CGN003
Revision Level: 1
Page 6 of 7

### 4.4  Personal Plans

The requirements of the overall Business Plan are achieved through the allocation of responsibilities to individual directors and managers for specific aspects of the Plan's performance. The method used is a combination of objectives set during the annual performance appraisal round coupled with the imposition of an incentive payment scheme related to the individual manager's achievement of revenue earning targets. For non-managers the commission plan is personal and not directly dependent on the performance of others; for directors and key managers performance payments are based on departmental performance.

In every case the compensation plan is generated on behalf of the Managing Director and is a direct requirement placed by him on the recipient of the plan.

### 5.0  Records and Reviews

Records of all planning activities will be retained until the plan to which they relate has been accepted and approved. There is no requirement to retain planning data after the approval of the plan unless this data must be retained for other reasons, for example for financial audit purposes.

Records of the performance of the plan will be generated as the business year proceeds as will records of personal performance through the year. These records, being part of the company's working records, will be retained so long as is necessary.

Performance of the business against the objectives set out in the plan will be monitored continuously with temporary and permanent records being generated as necessary. Each month the management team will review business performance and report this to the corporate HQ, with a more intensive review being conducted at the end of each quarter of the year.

At the end of each financial year the business performance will be reviewed and reported and will be closely linked to the production of the following year's Business Plan.

| | |
|---|---|
| **OMEGA UK LIMITED** | Document Number: CGN003 |
| | Revision Level: 1 |
| | Page 7 of 7 |

Annex 1

**OMEGA UK Business Plan – Sample Contents**

The sample contents of a typical business plan shown here are to be used as a guide in the absence of other directives. It is not necessarily an exhaustive list of contents, neither is the use of every heading mandatory for every occasion.

1   Management Summary

2   Objectives

3   Organisation

4   Revenue

5   Expenses

6   Marketing Plans

7   Customer Services Division

8   Training Plans

9   Summary

207

# Appendix 6

**Scope and purpose of the audit**

The purpose of this audit was to identify whether design control procedures are followed in relation to the design of training courses by the training group within Omega UK Ltd.

ISO9001 para 4.4 and the following company documents define the procedures used in Omega to achieve this purpose:

- DP13.1  Course design and verification
- DP13.2  Course documentation
- DP13.3  Course administration
- DP13.4  Course feedback and improvement
- DP13.7  Training needs analysis.

**Method**

The purpose of the audit was to assess whether the design process follows the documented procedures. Discussions before the audit indicated the main area requiring review was 'to ensure the course's programme is designed so it fulfils the requirements of the organisation for internal and external training'. The audit therefore concentrated on the procedures for analysing and fulfilling training needs.

**Observations**

Procedure DP13.7 in the training manual defines how the training group should gather information about the needs of users, and how this information is used to define the future training programme. This analysis may identify a need for changes to existing courses or a need for new courses.

The training department have set up an informal network of individuals which meets twice a year. The purpose of this committee is to ensure the training department meets their requirements as users. Minutes are recorded for this meeting. These demonstrate that the following topics were discussed in January 1995:

- Changes in the work profile
- Changes in the marketplace
- Changes in staff profile
- What individuals like and dislike about the existing programme.

The existence of this committee and the role it plays in defining training needs is not, however, included as part of the training procedures. It was also identified that not all users were represented on this committee (Recommendation 1).

In addition, the training department periodically review training needs by carrying out a formal training needs analysis. This is designed to identify what individuals do in the workplace, what do they do well and what they could do better. This is used to provide detailed training requirements. A comprehensive training needs analysis was performed in October 1995. This is the basis for the significant revision of the training programme for 1996. The training needs analysis has been documented, but the 1996 training programme has not yet been issued (Recommendation 2).

This training needs analysis also concentrates, almost exclusively, on internal training needs. External needs seem to be identified on an *ad hoc* basis based on inputs from the sales and marketing departments. This sometimes leads to external customer needs being identified that the training group cannot meet because its resources have already been committed (Recommendation 3).

Design changes to existing courses primarily come about as a result of course feedback. The training department asks each course attender to return an assessment for each course. These are summarised, analysed and used as a basis for making changes to the content of courses and to review the performance of presenters. The present system of recording assessments does not encourage attenders to give a separate assessment for the material and the presenter. It is, therefore, possible that changes to a course may be made when all that is required is a change in presentation techniques (Recommendation 4).

Having looked in detail at the inputs to the design department, we selected two new courses and looked at the design processes followed for each. These were a general course describing the service

210

requirements of the new instrument OI456 and a customer-specific course on conducting performance appraisals. Taking each of these in turn.

For the instruments course, the need and course requirements were defined in detail by the customer support department. In general the design control procedures were followed. The only exception was that, at the time the course was designed, the service manuals were not available. This led to some minor modifications to the course before it was released to tie up with the service manuals when they became available (Recommendation 5).

For the course on conducting appraisals, the input was received from the sales department. A formal contract review was carried out before the project was accepted. All the design control procedures were followed, including a customer verification, before the design was released for delivery. The course has already been run four times since release in September and has achieved customer ratings of a minimum of 4.8 each time. This equates to a rating of 'excellent'.

### Conclusions

The training department operates the prescribed system for designing training courses. The system conforms to the requirements of ISO9001 para 4.4. In general the design control procedures are being followed. The main area for improvement is in the methods used to ensure full identification of customer requirements and inputs. The following recommendations for improvement are made:

### Recommendations

1 The use of the training committee as a method of data collection should be formalised as it plays an important role in directing the training group.
2 The training programme resulting from the training needs analysis prepared in October should now be issued. The procedure DP13.7 should be amended to include a deadline for issuing the following year's programme. If the programme is issued late then personnel may not be able to attend the courses they require.

3 The procedure for carrying out the training needs analysis needs to be amended to ensure that all anticipated external needs are identified as well as the internal needs.

4 Assessment forms should include a box to record comments on the content of sessions and the presenter.

5 Omega International should ensure support manuals are available at product launch.

212

# Appendix 7

OMEGA INTERNATIONAL

**Audit Report 008/95**                                    **23rd February 1995**
Page 1 of 2

## Scope

The purpose of the audit is to determine whether material handling is being carried out in accordance with ISO9001 para 4.15 and the associated company procedures, standards and instructions.

## Location

All material reception, handling and storage areas.

## Auditor

J. Land: senior auditor, Omega International

## Purpose

This audit was conducted as part of the company's continuing audit of its quality system. Its purpose was to assess the adequacy of the material handling arrangements. This includes items supplied by external suppliers, internal handling arrangements and arrangements to prevent damage in transit.

## Method and observations

The audit was conducted with the co-operation of the stores manager, and the support staff within stores, production and packing.

As part of the audit process we examined the records of scrap and rework due to loss and damage during storage. We also examined the customer complaints file for records of damage reported on delivered product. Data from these sources, together with the findings of the factory audit are included in the audit conclusions.

The audit began with a review of the arrangements for establishing the packaging requirements and procuring the materials to meet these requirements. The company design manual requires that transit packaging be designed for each product as part of the design process.

During the production planning process, arrangements are then made to ensure the materials to meet these requirements are procured. There is, however, no requirement to specify and procure handling and storage materials to protect the product from damage during production and storage. This results in a shortage of suitable containers and packaging to prevent the product from damage in the factory (Observation 1).

We examined the operation of the despatch packing bay. There is evidence that the majority of products are packed according to the packing specification. There is, however, evidence that occasionally items are despatched using other packing materials than those specified. This is due to a shortage of space in the packing bay. Consequently only high-volume product packing materials are kept to hand. For low-volume products the material is not to hand and despatch personnel use the material they have to hand which nearest meets the requirements (Observation 2).

Examination of the storage areas was inconclusive. Examination of the factory records, however, indicated a high incidence of stores scrap and also the issue of items beyond their useful shelf life (Observation 3).

Office areas were visited, and it is here that there is major cause for concern. Items are removed from the production and stores areas to the design and sales offices. Whilst there it is not subject to control to prevent damage or loss. *If* the item is subsequently returned to production it is frequently returned without identification and without verification that it meets the requirements. We consider this to be a serious breach of the Standard and the company operating procedures (Observation 4).

**Conclusions**

Whilst generally conforming to the requirements of ISO9001 and the company operating procedures, a number of deficiencies were raised. The audit conclusions are contained in Annex 1 to this report, together with details of the actions agreed to rectify the audit deficiencies.

214

**OMEGA INTERNATIONAL**
**Audit Deficiency Report**
**Annex 1 to Audit Report 008/95**

*Observation 1*
Production engineering have embarked on a programme to identify the production and storage packing needs for existing products. These materials will be specified and procured by the material control group. The design manual is being amended to ensure that internal handling and packaging materials are specified during the design process for all new products. These actions will be completed by the end of April 1995.

*Observation 2*
Additional storage space adjacent to the packing bay has been made available to overcome the packing storage problem. Staff have also been trained in their responsibilities for ensuring that the packaging specifications are fulfilled without deviation.

*Observation 3*
Stores personnel have been required to carry out regular audits of stores stock to ensure any items past their shelf life are identified and removed. Material control will also ensure that purchase of these items will in future be carried out more frequently with smaller amounts being purchased. Stores and purchasing procedures are being amended to reflect these changes. This will be completed by the end of March 1995.

215

*Observation 4*
Production management have established a system to ensure that both removal and return of items from stores and production areas are fully controlled. This includes the requirement to verify all products before they are accepted for return. This system is currently being documented. This will be completed by the end of March 1995.

*Future action*
Based on the findings of the audit and the corrective actions being implemented, we believe that the system to ensure safe handling and packaging of products should be reviewed in advance of the next scheduled audit. Another audit of the packaging and handling arrangements will, therefore, take place in September 1995.

**Distribution**
Stores manager
Purchasing manager
Production engineering manager
Manufacturing manager
Design manager
Audit file

# Appendix 8

THE ALPHA GROUP
QUALITY POLICY

The management and employees of The Alpha Group are committed to providing our customers with what they want, first time, every time. To achieve this we require everyone to strive constantly to improve the quality of the products and services we supply.

*J. McGregor*

J. McGregor
President
The Alpha Group

# Appendix 9A

THE ALPHA GROUP – EXTRACT FROM GROUP STRUCTURE CHART

THE
ALPHA GROUP

Omega Instruments
Instrumentation
division

Omega International
design and
manufacture

Omega UK Ltd
UK sales, distribution
support and training

# Appendix 9B

OMEGA UK LTD – EXTRACT FROM MANAGEMENT STRUCTURE CHART

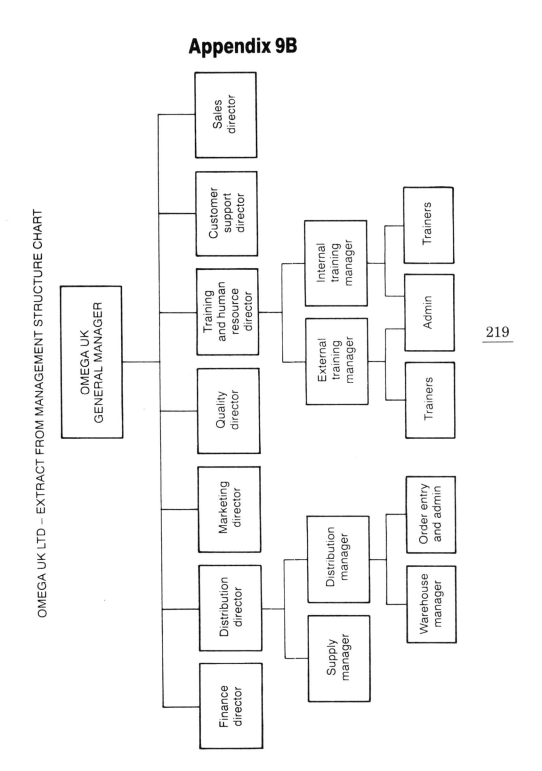

# Appendix 10

**OMEGA UK**                                      **TRAINING DEPARTMENT**

JOB DESCRIPTION – TRAINING DIRECTOR

---

**Responsibilities**

Reporting to the UK General Manager

- Define the objectives for the National Training department.
- Identify the training needs of the organisation and develop a training programme to meet those needs cost effectively.
- In conjunction with the marketing and sales departments, identify the training needs of external customers and develop a programme to meet those needs cost effectively.
- Manage the training department.
- Monitor the performance of training courses and ensure they remain of a consistently high quality.
- Administer the training programme.
- Develop a three-year plan to direct the development of training.
- Retain technical competence.
- Ensure at all times that the established procedures are followed to ensure customer requirements are met, at minimum cost to the organisation.

**Performance measures**

- Satisfactory customer service, both internal and external.
- Provision of the training programme within the budget constraints agreed.
- Management of the training organisation to ensure goals are met.
- Management of the staff within the training department. This includes development of a succession plan.
- Satisfactory audit results both from internal and external auditors.

**Resources**

Management of the following personnel and resources:
- Internal training manager and their team.
- External training manager and their team.
- Training budget as agreed with the general manager.
- Equipment and accommodation.

**Authority**

- To define the objectives of the Training department subject to approval by the general manager.
- Control budget spend in accordance with the agreed budget. Financial limit of £10K without the general manager's signature.
- Day-to-day supervision of staff, appraisal and counselling in accordance with established procedures.

Approved:    S. Baldwin, General Manager      *S. Baldwin*

Agreed:        G. French, Training Director      *G. French*

Date:           5th June 1995

# Appendix 11

## List of Accredited Independent Third-Party Certification Bodies

1. BSI Quality Assurance (BSIQA)
   Business Development
   PO Box 375
   Milton Keynes
   MK14 6LL        01908 220908

2. Lloyds Register Quality Assurance Ltd (LRQA)
   Hiramford
   Middlemarch Office Village
   Siskin Drive
   Coventry
   CV3 4FJ        01203 639566

3. Yarsley Quality Assured Firms Ltd (YQAF)
   Trowers Way
   Redhill
   Surrey
   RH1 2JN        01737 768445

4. The Loss Prevention Certification Board Ltd (LPCB)
   Melrose Avenue
   Borehamwood
   Herts
   WD6 2BJ        0181 207 2345

5. Bureau Veritas Quality International Ltd (BVQI)
   70 Borough High Street
   London
   SE1 1XF        0171 378 8113

6. Det Norske Veritas Quality Assurance Ltd (DNVQA)
   Veritas House
   112 Station Road
   Sidcup
   Kent
   DA15 7BU        0181 309 7477

7. Construction Quality Assurance (CQA)
   Arcade Chambers
   The Arcade
   Market Place
   Newark
   Notts
   NG24 1UD          01636 708700

8. National Inspection Council Quality Assurance Ltd (NQA)
   5 Cotswold Business Park
   Millfield Lane
   Caddington
   LU1 4AR          01582 841144

9. UK Certification Authority for Reinforcing Steels (CARES)
   Oak House
   Tubs Hill
   Sevenoaks
   Kent
   TN13 1BL          01732 450000

10. British Approvals Service for Cables (BASEC)
    Silbury Court
    360 Silbury Boulevard
    Milton Keynes
    MK9 2AF          01908 691121

11. Ceramic Industry Certification Scheme Ltd (CICS)
    Queens Road
    Penkhull
    Stoke on Trent
    ST4 7LQ          01782 411008

12. The Quality Scheme for Ready Mixed Concrete (QSRMC)
    3 High Street
    Hampton
    Middlesex
    TW12 2SQ          0181 941 0273

13. ASTA Certification Services
    23/24 Market Place
    Rugby
    Warwickshire
    CV21 3DU        01788 578435


14. SIRA Certification Service
    Saighton Lane
    Saighton
    Chester
    CH3 6EG         01244 332200


15. Associated Offices Quality Certification Ltd (AOQC)
    Longridge House
    Longridge Place
    Manchester
    M60 4DT         0161 833 2295

225

16. TRADA Quality Assurance Services Ltd
    Stocking Lane
    Hughenden Valley
    High Wycombe
    Bucks
    HP14 4NR        01240 245484


17. Engineering Inspection Authorities Board (EIAB)
    The Institution of Mechanical Engineers
    1 Birdcage Walk
    London
    SW1H 9JJ        0171 222 7899


18. Central Certification Service (CCS)
    Victoria House
    123 Midland Road
    Wellingborough
    Northamptonshire
    NN8 1LU         01933 441796

19. National Approval Council for Security Systems (NACOSS)
    Queensgate House
    14 Cookham Road
    Maidenhead
    Berks
    SL6 8AJ          01628 37512

20. Steel Construction QA Scheme Ltd (SCQAS)
    4 Whitehall Court
    Westminster
    London
    SW1A 2ES         0171 839 8566

21. Electrical Association Quality Assurance Ltd (EAQA)
    30 Millbank
    London
    SW1P 4RD         0171 828 9227

22. Water Industry Certification Scheme (WICS)
    Frankland Road
    Blagrove
    Swindon
    Wilts
    SN5 8YF          01793 410005

23. BMT Quality Assessors Ltd (BMTQA)
    Scottish Metropolitan Alpha Centre
    Stirling University Innovation Park
    Stirling
    FK9 4NF          01786 50891

# Index

■